NOWHERE TO GO

NAVIGATING TOUGH TRANSITIONS

NOWHERE TO GO

GEORGE KALANTZIS

NOWHERE TO GO
Navigating Tough Transitions

ISBN: 978-1-5445-2252-4 *Hardcover*
978-1-5445-2250-0 *Paperback*
978-1-5445-2251-7 *Ebook*

This is for us who want to run,
laugh, and play

For those who have forgotten we have
so much more to say

Thank you to all my mentors in life who
taught me to see the beauty in the world I am living.
For believing me in my darkest hours,
when I wasn't so forgiving

This is for my daughter, so she knows
how to follow her heart

It only takes a few words, and seconds
of courage to start

Contents

Acknowledgments

What you are about to read is a story I never thought possible.

I've met so many unique humans along my path, and this book wouldn't be possible without everyone who believed in me when I didn't believe in myself.

First, my writing mentor, John Romaniello. Not only did he help me reach my pinnacle during my training days, but he also helped me see that no matter how painful things were, my story wasn't over. And so, every morning I felt like running, I still wrote what I knew—nothing more, nothing less. After I finished an entirely different story than the one you see here, I asked John for advice. With his professional expertise and heartfelt guidance, he spent a few hours walking me through the actual story I needed to write. Which is the one you're about to read.

Second, Traver Boehm and the incredible men who had a tremendous impact on helping me see this book through to the final edits. Without Traver, I wouldn't be here today. He was with me on my darkest days. When I wanted to run, he helped me fight the hurt. Much of what I write and coach about comes from the concepts I learned from him and the unique people he introduced me to along the way. They are the foundation of who I am, and more importantly, the movement I am building.

Third, the men and women I served with during my decade as a Marine. My memories of you will forever be in my heart and soul. These words are for those who never made it back home. And for those who lost the battle with darkness. Your stories haven't faded into nothingness. Instead, they are the beacon of strength many need to survive.

Fourth, my family and friends who stuck by me during my darkest days. These words clear the path to our heart's center. Every tear I shed leaves a call for wholeness that connects us back to all of who we are. I have so much love for all of you.

And finally, I want to acknowledge the team at Scribe Media. Thank you for helping my vision come to life.

Essays and Poems

Moments

You will one day be able to look back and see this day was a defining moment for you

You may not see this right now because you are facing so many unknowns

But you will love, laugh, and smile again. I promise

Someday, you will tell your story

The challenges you faced did not crush your soul or break your heart

They made you open

Your voice matters

It always has

And so do you

Introduction

I don't know what stopped me the night I almost took
my own life. After more than a decade of running from
demons, I wanted it to be over. From childhood trauma and
severe depression to addiction and a devastating divorce,
I simply felt too broken, too exhausted to keep fighting.
And then, I did.

While I don't know exactly what it was, I can say God or something
greater out there saved my life. The same pull I'd felt all my life
that told me I was meant for something greater, showed up that
night. It told me that I wasn't even close to being done.

I believe every choice we make comes with consequences. If we
make choices to prove others wrong or that are fundamentally out
of alignment with what our heart tells us, then we will forever be
a slave to darkness.

It all started for me when I joined the Marine Corps in 2001. I remember asking myself, "What the fuck am I doing? What does it take to be the best? Can I push my body and mind past extreme discomfort when there's nothing left to give? Who am I?"

I've always been fascinated by the human mind and body. But I grew up in New Hampshire as the firstborn son in a divorced Greek family, which made self-exploration and individualization nearly impossible. I was told to *be a man*—a phrase so powerful that, it led to a lifetime of feeling like I was never good enough.

I knew my dad meant well. In the early years of my life, I cultivated a strong work ethic and the courage to seek something greater than myself. I knew that if I wanted to be part of something bigger, I had to do something extreme.

I joined the Marines to prove to everyone that I had what it took. Then the events of September 11, 2001 hit, and my quest for something greater than myself became abundantly clear. I was ready to move forward.

Of course, I didn't know what my future would be; all I knew was that something deep inside me was calling for me to be more. As my journey with the Marines began, I forged an identity that gave me the courage and strength needed to outlast the physical, mental, and moral battles I faced. As I climbed the ranks and gained valuable life experience, I believed that maybe it was true: perhaps each of us does have a unique reason for being here. Unfortunately, most of us never find the courage to trust ourselves enough to find what that is.

I wanted to retire from the Marine Corps at a certain point in my life. I pictured myself as the Marine who traveled the world, deployed to combat zones, and acted exactly like that badass you see in the movies. Instead, my years as a Marine consisted of death, addiction, and valuable life lessons that forced me to hang up my uniform after ten years of honorable service. When I left, I wasn't headed to an exotic location, surrounded by fellow Marines. I was on my way back home—a place I knew I'd never survive.

All those unresolved challenges I'd left behind ten years before were still in New Hampshire, waiting for me. I thought I'd outrun them, or at least put enough time between myself and my darker side. As it turned out, I hadn't. That's how I found myself lost, alone, and ready to end it all. Thankfully, my pull toward my life's calling was stronger than the darkness.

Writing my story has been scary, exhausting, cathartic, and freeing. The uncomfortable truth is that I needed all these experiences to find my calling. And that is what you'll read about in this book.

I think many of us are lost like I once was.

We forget that every choice we make comes with a consequence, even the ones we think are temporary or insignificant. Every moment we choose to hide in the shadows is a moment we lose ourselves in a sea of false beliefs. Those moments add up, one by one, until we're just a bunch of mindless bodies running around without direction or purpose.

I learned this the hard way. When I finally saw that my life was a direct reflection of everything I believed to be true about myself, I realized there was nowhere to go. The famous French-Cuban writer Anaïs Nin said, "We don't see things as they are, we see things as we are."

As you read these poems and essays from my life, see if you can locate the parts of yourself that called you here today. This is a reunion with the sides of you that have somehow been lost. The parts of you squeezed into a tiny box for choices in life that came with a cost.

Because Nin was correct in saying that our lives reflect everything we believe to be true about ourselves.

There's a reason we keep searching for a higher meaning in this relentless world. We all chase happiness. We all want deeper connections. We all want to look and feel good. We all want to be successful. These are all part of being human.

Unfortunately, many of us will never find the solution we seek. Not because there aren't enough answers, but because we're often caught up in the wrong chase and too blind to see that many of the things we crave are right in front of us.

To me, that is where the real work happens.

It happens in the moments when life presents you with unexpected challenges and all the things you thought were true yesterday are no longer true today. The vulnerability you feel as you step into the unknown will guide you away from your suffering and toward your true meaning.

This sounds cliché, and maybe it is, but I know that it applies to many of us.

Life is not linear. It's a magnificent dance that invites us to be and feel more than we could ever imagine. Tough transitions are where we realize what we're made of.

If you find yourself in a place where you feel lost, you must first learn to accept who you are underneath the chaos of life, to reach for something inside of you rather than outside of you. As you discover who you are underneath all the ways you've experienced life, you'll see that there is nowhere else to go. Liberation from your painful patterns begins by accepting everything you are.

I am not writing this book because I think I know it all or that I'm better than you. In fact, I know I'm probably worse. I have gone my entire life hiding behind masks and addicted to things that have caused harm, not only to myself, but to those closest to me. While I still have my doubts, I've learned that life is so much better when I remove my armor and own my story and my wounds.

The first step toward accepting my past was accountability. I had to take responsibility and face all the things I ran from my entire life. And that shit hurt. But I believe, there is immense power that comes from recognizing our own faults.

If you're anything like me, the first step for you will also hurt. It's uncomfortable and terrifying. There are so many unknowns. You'll probably feel stressed, anxious, and maybe even resort to your old habits. But, fight those urges. The beauty of the unknown is where you're going to find yourself—you'll find a way to be entirely different, better, even.

So, let's do this together. Let's come into alignment with ourselves, and commit to accepting all of who we are to unlock our inner mystery. Let's get intimate with our dark secrets that have shamed us and kept us from being our true selves. Let's break open those wounds from childhood, heartbreak, death, and any other moments where tough transitions challenged our life's story.

Please take a deep breath. Remember to open your heart to all the emotions that come to you throughout this book. When you reach the depths of your darkness, you will find the courage to own your story. If you can read these words with an open heart, you'll create new space to connect with the parts of you that led you here today.

You will no longer be driven by shame, guilt, fear, resentment, or even anger. Instead, you will find acceptance that something greater is happening at this very moment.

I know darkness well. The stories I'm about to share with you cover some of my most vulnerable moments in life. Like you, I've faced feelings of shame and regret, and repeated unhealthy patterns in my life until I hit rock bottom. Alone, and with no other options, I had no choice but to learn to pull myself back up.

I know what it feels like to want to reach into your past and change anything you could've done differently to erase all the events you wished didn't happen. But when we are in a place of "shoulds," we deny the path the Universe is trying to show us.

The purpose of my stories is to show you that you are not alone in this world. Whatever happened to make you feel lost couldn't have happened any other way. And while this idea might make you cringe, healing is never a fun process. Pain doesn't just disappear with time. When you learn to feel things as they come, you'll see that there is a plan for you, and this moment is part of that plan. It's time to stop resisting those uncomfortable truths, and start owning them.

If everything starts with a story, these words, paragraphs, and pages you are about to read will give you the power to free yourself from the heavy chains of the past. By sharing my journey with you, I too become free.

There are days when I struggle with doubt and fear and catch myself slipping into old patterns. The difference between me today and me yesterday is that I don't give up at the first sign of resistance. I know we are all in this place of uncertainty together. The lessons I write about go beyond who I am as a man. After all, if I am willing to step into the invitation life has given me, my words are a place to hold space and speak the truth for anyone else going through difficult times.

Maybe life isn't about achieving certain milestones, but rather a reflection of who we are as humans and how we show up in the world.

When we experience challenges that force us into the unknown, it's easy to hold on to whatever we have because it is familiar. **But I'm here to remind you that your life is unfolding the way it was intended for you if you trust your path and heart.** The more you trust yourself, the more you can listen, feel, and pay attention to the new life in front of you. I know it's hard to trust yourself in the unknown. But there will come a day when you look back and say this is the moment everything changed—all because you had the courage to keep going.

When we are done telling ourselves bullshit stories, we begin to see life through a different lens. We finally get to be ourselves, and with that comes extreme power. This is how you move from an abstract world that keeps you stuck in the past, to a vivid world that manifests everything you are worthy of.

I won't offer answers in the form of a five-step plan, or a precise method to follow. We are each unique, and our challenges are too personal for that. I will, however, offer my story. One that you can use to learn from, one that I hope will guide you to rise from your darkest times. By telling my story, I'm hoping that you will be able to imagine a better future for yourself.

I hope you find bits and pieces of yourself that give you the courage to take responsibility for the life you deserve. Many of our darkest times are not easy to revisit. You might not be ready to go back down that road, or even like what you find. But the stories and beliefs you currently hold about your way of life are the exact ones preventing you from awakening your power within.

This book is simply a tool to help you see yourself, honestly, for the first time. I hope to help you connect deeper with yourself, so you don't detach from your life's story, like I did. I can't force you to have uncomfortable conversations, face your fears, or show up. I can't even promise that you'll relate to everything in my story. However, I can share with you that it wasn't long ago that I felt utterly lost and hopeless, and that for me, losing everything created a life filled with sobriety, creativity, happiness, and love.

I encourage you to break free from the life you think you need to live, so you can create space for the one meant to unfold. Place your hands on your heart when you are tired and exhausted. Breathe in when you feel like you have nothing left.

Not only will you continue to be challenged, but you need to be. We go through transitions again and again to make us more open to the world, to allow us to step into the best version of ourselves. Give yourself permission to stop running. When you can do this, you'll see that you are worthy of everything you desire.

FREEDOM

Can you feel something that led you here to read this book?

There are parts of you that you must face

No going back. Breathe deep. Take a look

Transitions in life may have brought you to your knees

Today they are the catalyst to something greater as these words
   give you the courage to find what you need

Give yourself permission to sit here and take care of your heart

The parts that feel resentment from what was once torn apart

The shame and ridicule you felt when you were young

The child inside of you that was told to hold your tongue

The heaviness you feel from darkness and death

A necessary reminder that everything takes a last breath

What you desire in life is fundamentally yours to own

The resistance you feel is your calling to trust yourself in
the unknown

This is a reunion for the sides of you that have somehow
been lost

The parts of you squeezed into tiny boxes for choices in life
that came with a cost

Listen closely to the words that I am about to speak

No matter what you feel, keep trusting the rhythm of my beat

Every word creates a story to the path you must seek

The truth you will find is what makes your story unique

On these pages, you can give yourself permission to surrender to
the beauty of life that needs to unfold. Freedom from your
suffering comes from feeling your pain and letting go.

If you release the past, you can move forward with your heart

Don't rush the process, this is your life, you can always restart

Transitions

It's a strange place to be in life when you accept yourself for the first time. Writing about how I feel is still foreign to me; it makes me wonder how the fuck I ended up where I am today. But I have learned to take responsibility for this pain I feel, and so can you.

These stories are the battle between my inner and outer worlds, the stormy seas of my past. Each essay and poem is a wave that provides context for the need to go deeper into places I've run from my entire life.

I usually never took the time to slow down and feel the things I needed to feel. My teenage years consisted of seeking approval and validation with substance abuse. I ran away to the Marine Corps, only to morph to others' expectations while losing myself even further. I battled with the man in the mirror because I never believed I was worthy of life, which caused a battle with death itself.

All of these experiences have taught me that we have nowhere to go in life.

Your feelings will either take you in the direction of your heart or toward a life of emptiness and excuses. You cannot do both, so you must choose wisely.

With every transition in life, if we never take the time to accept what we feel and the experiences for what they are, we'll stay in a perpetual state of unhealthy patterns and become slaves to our past.

You can try to become someone or something else, which might make you feel better in the moment. You can find substances, relationships, and careers to numb what you don't want to face. But resisting the feelings that come with life transitions is a choice that keeps you forever stuck in a world that doesn't allow you to escape.

I'm not judging your feelings. I know what it feels like to navigate tough transitions when everything feels heavy. I'm telling you that you're not broken. Your pain needs to be seen, heard, and witnessed because the only way out of what you're facing is to work through it.

There is something about every tough transition that can ignite a flame of passion for finding your voice and emerging stronger than ever. It's freeing when you finally realize your story never ends, but rather you pick up a pen and write another chapter.

⁓

This is who I am, not who I was

or who I will be. Darkness

can't keep up. My words

set me free.

Nowhere to Go

The three best decisions I ever made came from places of hardship: the day I joined the Marines, the day I left, and the day I filed for divorce. These decisions all challenged my life story in complete, fundamental ways. It was as if the Universe wanted to suspend me in the unknown to see what I would make of it. These challenges forced me to choose between darkness and love. I had to choose my truth in order to move past these obstacles.

I could have kept running, coming up with excuses not to stop and reflect on my life. But realizing I had nowhere to go is how I found my true self. If we can't face the reflection in the mirror, then it's doubtful that anyone else wants to either.

Life is about learning how to accept and surrender to a full spectrum of experiences. There are no right or wrong ways to do this. The only thing that changed my life was opening up to the idea that I'm the only one responsible for changing what happens next.

Each of us has different interpretations of the truths that unfold in our lives. We hold certain truths to be so important that we refuse new information that doesn't align with our expectations. We apply our idea of truth to the events in our lives because it gives us a sense of control. But the truth can't be limited to what we want. Truth is all encompassing, and the longer you avoid accepting the broader truths of your life, the longer you will live inauthentically.

You keep every wound you refuse to heal, and you can never run fast enough to escape the effects of your past. You carry every painful memory with you in your journey until you find the courage to own your life's story. You might think you have control, but if your behaviors and choices don't match what you feel inside, you'll continue to send confusing messages to the world, and your life will reflect an empty image in the mirror.

Alan Watts, a British philosopher and writer known for his teachings on meditation, said, "To remain stable is to refrain from trying to separate yourself from a pain because you know that you cannot. Running away from fear is fear, fighting pain is pain, trying to be brave is being scared. If the mind is in pain, the mind is pain. The thinker has no other form than his thought. There is no escape."

To me, Watts means that we can find much of what we seek in our lives by accepting all of who we are. **We all have dark times**

in life. This is when we must do some serious reflection, dig deeper, and find the courage and strength we need to move through the challenges we face.

Far too many of us are desperately seeking answers to problems in life. We try to fill the void we feel with external possessions, experiences, or frivolous relationships. What most of us fail to understand is that those things end up creating more darkness.

As the pastor David Crosby said, "To suffer, that is common to all. To suffer, smile, and keep your composure, that is remarkable. Suffering shapes your perception of life, your values, priorities, goals, and dreams. Your pain is changing you."

Or to put it more simply: the pain we feel in life is an act of self-empowerment.

Unexpected life changes are fucking scary. I thought I had seen it all, but nothing compared to seeing the woman I thought I would spend the rest of my life with, in love with someone else. I felt like I was robbed of my life. The loss shook up my entire identity, and something dark inside me pulled me into a bottomless pit of despair.

I became a slave to darkness for nearly two decades. Dark thoughts at three a.m. were normal for me, and I developed an intimate relationship with death's presence over me. Typically, I'd wake up and get a hard training session in or numb the pain with alcohol and sex. But the cold, rigid fingers of darkness suffocated those spaces in my body that needed to breathe, and I had nowhere to go.

Darkness wasn't there to take my life, but rather to show me that all the places I ran to in order to escape were no longer options. My wounds were real, but they are not who I am. *Suddenly, I realized the darkness wasn't an outside force. It was the unexplored parts of me that I'd been afraid of for years. Knowing I could never outrun something I carried inside me, I found myself staring at the blank pages of a journal, writing frantically in the early hours of the morning.*

Darkness has come, and I do not know why,
I walk with him as he hears my cry.

Where we will go, I ask as he turns to me
and points into the unknown.

My pen bled out on the empty pages, and each word freed me from the chains of my past as I clashed with parts of me that needed to be free. Rather than resist life, I gave myself permission to feel everything that came to wrap itself around me. Every word I wrote and every breath I took gave me the courage to let my heart lead, even with the things that hurt the most.

I'm not sure how I got to that point in my life. All I know is that I fought long and hard in the unknown to learn I couldn't predict what would happen when faced with unexpected change; I could only discover what the Universe presented before me.

It's so easy to run from our pain and try to wish it away, but time does not heal all wounds. The real relief we all search for comes from understanding that we can experience sadness and grief and still look forward to a better future. Embracing our pain allows us to build the resiliency necessary to meet our true, whole self, even if the brighter future we're headed toward is not yet identifiable.

I hope I can help you see that your pain is an invitation to claim and heal yourself. Don't run; instead, take time to slow down and ask yourself what this experience wants from you. I avoided confronting my feelings for years. I wore emotional armor forged by my identity as a Marine. Today, when the shadows of the past call me, I get curious because I know I have work to do.

Any time I move closer to the shadows, a more fascinating, energizing story of my life emerges. When my hometown became too much to bear, I found the courage to join the Marines. When staying in the Marines became safer, more stable, I knew it wasn't for me. So, I left and started an entirely different career, filled with experiences I'd never have if I'd stayed comfortable.

My decision to file for divorce was incredibly painful. But it was nowhere near as painful as living in misery. Even writing this book, with all its reminders of my painful past, was an opportunity for me. I became a better person, and have hopefully created a better experience for you. Each time I stepped toward the darkness, I forced myself to make the right decision instead of allowing fear or thoughtless actions to take control of my story.

Your life and the pain you experience are unique. You have the choice to grieve and move through transitions in your own way even if others don't like it. Those choices will lead you to a life that is completely yours, consequences and all. This may seem scary, especially if you're not in the habit of taking responsibility for the consequences of your actions. But it's the only way to create the life you need to thrive.

Moments after a higher power saved my life, I decided I was no longer a slave to other people's lives or the limitations and stories that held me hostage. Through my pain, I created a new story, one that gave me the courage to open my heart and clear space for whatever needed to move through me. My path was not easy, but it was worth it for the freedom I enjoy today.

My calling unfolded in front of me the moment I formed a new relationship with the events of my life. I saw the value of slowing down and evaluating every piece of my life. Every morning, I returned to feel what lurked in the cave of darkness. For the next few months, I asked myself, "What can I find if I stay a bit longer?"

What a surprise: surrendering to my pain and choosing to purge unhealthy coping mechanisms freed up time and energy to focus on becoming a better man and father. With an open heart, I surrounded myself with people on a similar path. I signed up for men's groups, found mentors, went to retreats, tried martial arts, and started writing. It was the happiest and healthiest I'd felt in a long time and how I began to write this book.

I believe many of us have left parts of ourselves in search of something beyond ourselves to fill what we feel is lacking. The discomfort we feel and the alienation we sense from life are parts of us trapped between the past and future, far from the present.

As a result, we live in a place of emptiness because we have become distant from ourselves. We may not even recognize this until one day we don't know who we are or what we want from our lives. Once we can become more mindful of what we feel, however, we can see that we don't need anything outside of ourselves because what we need always comes from within.

Simple, right? Well, as with most things worth having in life, accepting that there is nowhere to go in your life is one of the hardest things to do. Many of us get stuck in the story we've told ourselves. We focus on what's happened to us instead of focusing on what we've decided for ourselves. Those stories, and the masks we wear to tell them, push our true selves further and further away. The result? Walking through life guarded and isolated.

As you read these words, pause for a moment. Close your eyes and take a deep breath to land here in the essence of it all. See if you can focus on your feelings a little longer. When you want to run, come back here and decide to lead with your heart first.

While acceptance might make you feel lost, if you can find the courage to sit with these feelings a little longer each day, you will find wisdom from your wounds. Most of them will have value and meaning if you are willing to release your past and move forward with your heart.

Over an entire year, I lost myself in the thoughts of yesterday and tomorrow. I felt parts of my body speak to me in a foreign language. I cried. I got sick. I wrote . . . a lot. But none of that mattered because the only way through one of my most challenging transitions was to surrender to life itself.

Once I accepted I had nowhere to go, I found a men's group that supported me when darkness came along my bedside, creeping up the walls. We inspired each other, and they encouraged me to lean into the darkness rather than run from it. The only way through was to let my heart bleed out in these pages before you. They showed me how to believe in something greater than my pain because I felt seen, heard, and witnessed for the first time in my life.

These men understand how hard it is to stay connected to their true selves when life knocks them down and why living with an open heart is one of the hardest things we can do. They are the true warriors in life. In fact, I would argue that finding the courage to own your pain is more rewarding and challenging than any physical feat you could ever accomplish.

Taking responsibility for your life is not, and never will be, easy. It's even more difficult if you've spent a lifetime believing stories that limit your potential. But we've seen what happens when we don't take control of our own life. We walk around feeling unworthy, unseen, and unappreciated. I want to remind you that every day we are granted the gift of life is a chance for us to begin again.

In truth, losing everything was the best thing that ever happened to me because I had to look at life from a different perspective. I had to stop running. I had to accept my entire story and take full responsibility for my life, and I needed to hit rock bottom to get there. You may not need to hit rock bottom to write another chapter in your life, but there is something powerful about those moments when we are challenged to go against everything we've been taught. When we stop being the victim of our life and become the creator, we often find what we are looking for.

The Places I've Gone

My life began with a challenge to rise from the moment I was born. As the firstborn son in a Greek family, I was given my pappoús (grandfather's) name. This tradition binds you to your Greek heritage and ties the family together for generations. Like so many of us, I crafted an identity throughout my childhood. Mine came with a lot of shame and the need to continually prove myself worthy in everything I did.

My dad was a traditional Greek man: exceptional work ethic, family man, and kind of a straight edge. My mom was the complete opposite: rebellious and fiery, she lived life to the fullest. Much of my childhood was a blur, but one key event stuck with me.

I remember riding my bike home from school when I was six and seeing my mom throwing clothes out the windows. As I peddled closer, I could hear her screaming at my dad. I had no idea what was going on. The only thing I knew was that a few days after this fight, men in suits came to our house and took everything away. Suddenly, my life took an unexpected turn, and I had no control over the situation. I felt broken inside.

It felt like my parents had abandoned me. They were physically still around, but they were so caught up in their own issues, that they forgot their actions affected us kids too. My hopes and dreams as a little boy were shot down that afternoon.

Despite my feelings, I knew what was expected of me as a young man. I wanted to show my dad I could handle the change, so I held back my tears and refused to let anyone see my hurt. I tried to convince myself that their split didn't hurt me. Consequently, my relationship with my parents was never the same, and neither was my life. To this day, everyone thinks it was the Marines that helped me develop a resilient mind. But I think it started much earlier, as a young boy navigating these hardships.

After the divorce, my dad was awarded full custody of me, my older sister, and my little brother. I'm a Greek boy, so I followed the family lead. At eight, I worked for the family restaurant as a busboy and discovered the meaning of hard work and discipline. Sports didn't interest me, so I chose to work throughout much of my childhood. I didn't know this at the time, but the standards imposed on me while working so young set a precedent for extremely high expectations. For decades, those expectations would be a constant driver throughout my years of hidden shame.

By the time I was in middle school, my dad remarried and had more kids. Nearly every memory I have of my dad involves him working long hours to provide for the family. I admired his hard work, but he was a lost soul held hostage by his own past.

My relationship with my mother is blurry. She was a single mom on government support for most of my childhood. For many of those years, she was emotionally distressed. Often, she was too distracted by her own worries to respond to the needs of a young boy. Without the love and support I needed from my mom, I started to look elsewhere to fill the void. I felt responsible for what happened, and their chaos became mine.

By high school, the quiet kid in class wasn't so quiet anymore. I looked for ways to get my needs met. I hung out with a crowd that influenced me to skip class, binge drink, and sell drugs. I quickly forged an identity of confidence, fake as it was. I didn't care what happened to me or how far I pushed the rules. All that mattered was that I found ways to prove to everyone but myself that I was worthy.

Everything changed after the attacks of September 11, 2001. I suddenly had a purpose, one that didn't involve parties or breaking the law. In fact, I chose an entirely opposite lifestyle. I found something greater than myself in the Marines.

Becoming a Marine was one of the proudest moments of my life. I felt as if something unlocked in me. I thought I'd found my purpose, and was going to war. As it turned out, the Universe had a different plan for me. One that would challenge my entire psyche.

My time in the Marines wasn't what I'd imagined. In the first few years after graduation, I lost my best friend in the Iraq War. The battle to find out who I was as a man spiraled out of control with addictive behaviors. I carried the weight of his death on my shoulders for over ten years.

I couldn't recognize it at the time, but the years I spent in the military were a mirror image of my teenage years. This time, instead of selling drugs and partying, I buried my feelings in stoicism and excessive pride. I became hypervigilant to how others perceived me and developed an internal dialogue so dark that suicidal thoughts became a regular occurrence. It's not that I wanted to die; it was more the idea of death became a reality because we were all warriors.

It takes a different breed of human to become a Marine. Anything that gets you to find an uncommon willingness to fight for something greater than yourself does. But the Marines creates warriors with a survival mindset. This meant I was willing to accept certain things, like death. After a while, I developed an ambivalent feeling toward suicide. A warrior's death is an honor; I was okay with dying if it meant I could die for something bigger than myself.

The choices I made in the Marines left me vulnerable to the idea that I was never enough. I clung to the idea that my self-worth came from my achievements. And despite all I accomplished, I still felt like it was never enough. When it was time to hang up my uniform for the last time, I was alone and scared, and I clung tightly to my warrior identity while other parts of me slowly faded away.

Here's why this matters: my decision to leave the Marines was not what I originally intended. Before my last deployment to Afghanistan, I found myself drunk at the wheel one night and ended up with a DUI. I felt like a failure and a disgrace to the uniform. I was proud of my time in the service, but I carried a great deal of shame from this incident, and I chose to leave on my terms rather than sit around the ranks with that much shame.

After a decade of service, there wasn't anyone to bond over the pain, blood, and sweat. Though I wasn't sure what would come next, one thing was certain: I wasn't ready to face myself, and I didn't know how to sit in the discomfort. So I defaulted to what I always did—run.

I took what seemed like the most logical route after leaving the military. I applied for MBA programs in the hope of finding something greater than myself again. But it wasn't long before I found myself with restless nights, memories of my friend killed by a roadside bomb in Iraq, and heavy drinking. I thought I'd put my past behind me, but there it was, waiting for the next opportunity to reveal its pain.

I wondered if my pain would ever go away. I felt like something inside me was missing, so I took a contract job in Afghanistan with some friends from the military to feel that sense of purpose again.

I was twenty-eight years old, no longer a Marine, but in a place that made me feel safe. From the outside looking in, I imagined it looked like a success. From the inside looking out, it was dark and gruesome.

Back home in New Hampshire, my girlfriend, Shawna, who would later become my wife, had no idea I felt like this. No one did. Shawna and I fell in love fast. She was always there for me and supported me in any way possible. But I ignored this support because I never felt worthy of love itself. All I could do was focus on the pain I felt and wish away the darkness in my place of deep suffering.

It was a vicious cycle that never seemed to leave my sight. The reality is, no matter how hard I wanted to fight it, my past wasn't gone; it was right there behind my emotional armor. **Because the past doesn't just walk away from you. It is so powerful; I can understand why so many people want to run from it. It follows you until you find the courage to stop running.**

The hardest thing about being here today is that these shadows find their way into my life any chance they get. I don't know if they're here to protect me or harm me, but they never go away.

Who wants to admit they're controlled, not by their thoughts, but by events that happened years ago? Usually, what we see when we confront ourselves is a direct connection between our biggest conflicts and our biggest fears from the past.

Shame drove for what I didn't like about myself, and every choice I made came from an attempt to heal the emotional wounds I'd covered up my entire life. I spent a considerable amount of time avoiding and minimizing situations that needed me to be vulnerable. It was as if someone else had infiltrated my relationships to sex, love, money, and happiness. I wasn't in control of my choices or my life story. Something had to change.

The first step was getting curious about the patterns in my life. I took an inventory of all my unhealthy coping mechanisms that weren't serving me. Drinking, sex, and other vices topped the list, so I chipped away at those behaviors. I chose a life of sobriety, celibacy, and creative expression rather than defaulting to the choices I make when I'm desperate to fill the silence as soon as possible.

Taking inventory of my life and my choices revealed so much to me. I began to understand my patterns, my triggers, and who I was underneath all the hidden layers. Knowing myself, genuinely —rather than knowing the man wearing the mask—gave me the tools I needed to grow. They help me handle uncomfortable situations without running from my feelings.

Whenever you face transitions in life, your pain will follow you, no matter how hard you try to push it away. We tend to only see and hear what we want to believe. But willful ignorance is only a temporary solution to our pain and unresolved wounds. It won't last. We won't last that way.

I believe we all have moments when we have no choice but to reckon with the defining moments of our lives. Most of us will be adults trying to process the events of our childhood in these moments. There will be layers, decades of hurt, unhealthy behavior, and shame. It'll be easier to ignore the moment or numb it with a coping strategy.

If we choose to get curious about everything we run from, we can see how the past seeps into our lives in all kinds of hidden ways.

These days I have slowed way down. Rather than start the day numbing my sense of shame with aggressive workouts and criticism to those closest to me, I wake up and do a body scan check. I don't keep my phone in my room for this reason. I'm not distracted by the thoughts of yesterday or tomorrow, but rather I focus on how I feel right when I wake up.

With my feet on the ground, I take a deep breath and thank the Universe for granting me another breath. Then I make my bed and proceed to make a hydration cocktail filled with pink Himalayan salt and lime juice. I then make my way over to my meditation cushion and sit down in silence. The stillness of my breath allows me to check in with my body on a deeper level. When I am finished with my meditation, I sit my ass down to write.

While writing this book, I came face-to-face with the harsh inner critic that drove me to seek such high intensity in my life. There were many days when I wanted to run. It was easier for me to fight and hold onto this aggressive side than to be vulnerable. But every morning I fed this dark side of me what he wanted. Rather than going faster, I went deeper. I took the time to develop a relationship with this side of me and reframe my need to protect my honor by redirecting my energy to something that had a purpose.

Learning more about what I was scared to openly express and how I projected my trauma onto others was a necessary step to opening up my heart to the world. Most importantly, it made room for me to build an incredible relationship with my daughter.

She reminds me of the simplicity in life. The more I watch her grow, the more my love for her transforms the wounds from my past. At the end of the day, I know the work I'm doing isn't just for me, but it's for her too.

My daughter shows me that life is no longer about me. I am about life. I'm in a new chapter where I recognize that I have the power to choose a new future. I've always looked up to fathers who have a strong bond with their children. Seeing their relationship with the world is beautiful, and I never had that. There are plenty of people who complain about spending time with their children, and I used to be one of them, but I do my best not to associate with them now and remove that negativity from my life.

It's an exciting place to be because, while I do have my days of anger and frustration with my little one, I've been able to see the invitation life has given me. The shifts I've experienced in life, while painful, are revelations that have allowed me to step into the most authentic version of myself.

Swiss psychiatrist Carl Jung said, "I am not what happened to me, I am what I choose to become." I think what he meant is that our story in life is never set in stone. While we cannot abandon our past, accepting all of who we are allows us to form a new set of beliefs and create a new chapter in life.

This is my life, and I share it not to persuade anyone to change but to give you an example of what happens when you begin to take responsibility for your life rather than run from it.

You have the power to change your entire lineage by breaking the mold.

So, while I'm here, in the same place my parents were over thirty years ago, I'm choosing to say that it stops with me. And this is where my freedom lies.

❧

I was told to grow up

and be a man by many

lost souls. Protection mechanisms

stamped on their hearts. Never

happy, I suppose. A lost, lonely

boy, the battle with my demons

began. Through the eyes of a

troubled teenager, addictions I ran.

Permission to Fail

I have nostalgic memories of being a high school kid during the '90s and trying to fit in. When I started my freshman year, I was exposed to a hierarchy of social crowds that left me wondering where I would end up. Jocks, preps, stoners, comedians, and goths left me negotiating my sense of self.

At first, I wasn't too impressed by the groups. This was probably because I was still working for my family after school and hung out with childhood friends. Plus, the classes were challenging enough to keep me engaged during class. But by the end of freshman year, after a year on the honor roll and trying out for all sorts of sports teams, my interest in getting good grades quickly came to a halt. I had to figure out a way to be a cool kid instead of a quiet, smart kid.

Isn't that how most of our lives go? **We create stories in our heads about why we aren't good enough and choose a life based on validation and approval-seeking behaviors.**

Accepting myself at the age of sixteen wasn't an option, so to avoid any fears of being a loser, I asked my uncle for a job at his tanning salon. The only condition he had was I would go to school, have a B average, and participate in sports. I had A's and B's at the time, so I took the job and soon started lying to him when my grades fell.

Skipping classes to work became a daily routine: I'd show up for attendance in the morning, take my first few classes, ditch early, get high, then go to work. I wasn't concerned with what I was doing because I had a plan. After graduation, I'd work for the family business. I'd already done it as a kid, and it sounded like the adult thing to do, so why not? I set myself on the same autopilot that most teenagers do. I focused on money and making as many friends as possible.

But in junior year, I got into drugs and alcohol. At first, it was a few parties here, a joint there, and a beer or two like most teenagers did in the '90s. I never stopped to think about whether I wanted to do any of these things or not. The only thing I cared about was fitting in. It didn't take long before I started experimenting with ecstasy (MDMA) and getting caught up with the wrong crowd. On the weekends, my uncle would go away and leave me and my cousins to run his business. That's when I began to get reckless and throw parties at the salon. It was the perfect spot, until it wasn't.

Word got out about the exclusive parties, and before I knew it, things got out of hand. I was hiding hundreds of pills under my mattress, in my shoes, and anywhere else I could squeeze a ten pack to sell at my parties. I even hid drugs in a secret locker at school. Every weekend, these raves would bring me thousands of dollars in drug sales. I was consumed by the entire culture for years. To this day, I don't know how I made it out of those years alive, and without a record. I was hanging out with people who had no plans for the future. Some of them were well into their young adult years, and others were my age. At seventeen years old, I had no goals, guidance, or any real plan. I should have asked for help. I should have tried harder and taken my life more seriously. But that's not how it happened, and I'm not sure I'd be who I am today without those chaotic years.

That summer going into senior year, I experienced one of the most radical changes in my life.

During a carnival in August, I found myself in front of a Marine Corps recruiting booth. At the time, I had absolutely no clue what I was doing. All I cared about was what others thought of me. In this case, it turned out to be a good thing, because it drove me to brag a little on the chin-up bar. I got seven and walked away proud with a card in my pocket that promised a future.

I had gotten used to the kids my age talking about colleges, while I felt like a failure. When my family asked about my plan, they were okay with me working in the family business because that's what Greeks do. I think my dad knew something was wrong, but

I never had the heart to tell anyone what was really going on in my life. I didn't want to admit what I was feeling, that failure was on my mind constantly. So I did something about it. It turned out to be one of the best decisions in my life. Rather than let failure define who I was, I decided to make something from it and found myself in the Marine Corps recruiter's office. Only there were a few things I had to take care of first.

I needed to back down from selling drugs and actually graduate high school. Both were not going to be easy. Backing out of selling drugs isn't as simple as quitting a regular job, especially when you're one of the top sellers for a major player in the drug world. Luckily, working for my uncle taught me a few things about negotiation and hustle. I worked out a deal too good to pass on, and I was done selling drugs within the first few weeks of my senior year.

My second obstacle was graduation. The Marines couldn't do much for me if I didn't have enough credits. So, even though I was in no condition to pass the initial fitness test required to join the Marines, nor had I told my parents the truth about my plan for the future, I focused on my grades. I believed in something greater than myself and knew my future was out there. I had to be willing to work hard, be honest with myself, and go after it.

I joined a gym, ran to and from school, and even told my teachers and the principal about my choice to join the Marines. As hard as I worked, though, it wasn't enough. The school told me I'd have to repeat my senior year, delaying my dream of joining the Marines at least another year. Then it was the morning of September 11, 2001. The world changed in the blink of an eye.

I was in English class when the monitors turned on with an announcement that America was being attacked. At first, all we saw were images of smoke and fire exploding out of one of the tallest buildings in New York. Then seconds later, I witnessed a plane sweep across the screen's edges, crashing into the other tower. My life and millions of others' lives would never be the same. America was going to war.

I will never forget leaving school early to go to the recruiter's office. It was the most prideful I'd ever felt. I replaced my fear of failure with an urgency to act without even knowing I was doing it. It turns out, that was the momentum I needed to give me a sense of purpose in life.

I sat down with my principal and teachers to develop a plan to graduate. There was a renewed sense of urgency; everyone knew I couldn't wait a full year before serving our country. Their ability to create a path forward for me taught me that no matter how lost you feel, there is always hope. And hope is all you need to find your way through the difficult challenges of the world.

I was assigned to morning and evening detention, plus doubled up on classes to make up for the credits needed to graduate. I trained for boot camp every day. There were no exceptions to the rules if I wanted to be a Marine. If I missed a class or skipped detention, I wouldn't graduate and have the chance to become a Marine. The challenge was not to give up when life seemed hopeless. I realized it wasn't a failure if I had a different path than everyone around me. I was working toward something different, something meant for me, and that made me successful, in my own way.

My senior year went by fast. Fortunately, I ended up graduating. I was the first person in my family to have a diploma. Within a few weeks, I shipped off to boot camp and realized some of life's defining moments are found by overpowering your desire to give in to fear.

At eighteen, I learned one of the most valuable lessons I've ever learned, but it took almost twenty years for it to sink in.

Many of us let the fear of failure run our lives. We stick to a predetermined script for how life is supposed to go and what our achievements should look like. We cling to these norms to avoid disappointment. But I believe that our most radical shifts in life come from giving ourselves permission to fail.

That's the test we all face because the most demanding challenges are won when we accept that we never need to have life all figured out; we just need to be willing to give ourselves permission to trust ourselves when we feel lost.

It's important to feel like an outsider. It's essential to feel the pain from an unexpected life change. Most people will do everything they can to avoid being looked at like a failure, even if it means rejecting their happiness and self-worth. That's not living life, that's existing. Your challenge is to make sure you're always living.

Giving yourself permission to fail will be uncomfortable. Your mind will tell you to stop and conform to the expectations of others. It's easy to beat yourself up when transitions in life find you. But trust yourself to go deeper. Life will always find a way to make you come face- to-face with the unknown. Take the leap into the unknown. Trust yourself to fail many times in life. Turning toward your fear of failure will give you the strength and courage to find light when darkness comes.

I know this because I have faced many hardships since graduating high school. But every time I was on the verge of quitting, the teenage boy who overcame his obstacles began shouting, "Give yourself permission to fail!"

Failure, then, propels us forward because we recognize that we are responsible for our lives. We step into power, where we can create any life we want.

I am not broken.

I am not lost.

I am here, right now.

In this moment, everything

unfolds, and the world

adjusts to who I want to be.

Life Is Earned,
Never Given

You never know the level of strength and courage you have inside until you have something greater than yourself to fight for.

The day I stepped on the yellow footprints at Marine Corps Paris Island was one of the most defining moments in my life. With my fists clenched and my thumbs along my pant seams, spit came across my forehead as a drill instructor yelled at me to lock my body. For the next ninety-six hours, the only words I spoke were "yes sir, no sir, and aye-aye sir."

As I quickly walked through two large silver doors, the drill instructor in front of us yelled, "You can only pass through these doors once in your life! Thereafter, you must enter and exit from a different door."

When those large silver hatches closed behind me, one chapter of my life ended, and so too, did another one begin.

That passage represents a recruit's official entrance into becoming a Marine. No one else walks through those large silver doors. It's a tradition and a commitment to accept the challenge in a collective effort to rise to something greater. The result is becoming part of an elite breed of humans fueled by a common bond like no other.

I almost forgot about this rite of passage. Then I sat down to write this book, and I was reminded of what I endured almost twenty years ago.

Tough transitions present you with the opportunity to walk through your own silver doors. You only get to pass through the challenges in front of you once, so choose your path wisely.

Joseph Campbell wrote about this idea in his book *The Hero with a Thousand Faces*. He says, "The agony of breaking through personal limitations is the agony of spiritual growth. Art, literature, myth and cult, philosophy, and ascetic disciplines are instruments to help the individual past his limiting horizons into spheres of ever-expanding realization."

Campbell explains that we are the hero in our own journey, and our lives reflect what we believe to be true about ourselves. We often want one thing but choose another because of society's rules or what we think is required of us to be successful adults. We end up with a life that just happens to us rather than something we consciously choose. This is a total mindfuck because it goes against almost everything we've been taught about life.

The hero's journey is called a journey for a reason: beliefs and choices are threaded together in the fabric of life. Every choice leads to another, and any attempt to escape from the uncomfortable beliefs you have about yourself will only lead to choices that keep you forever stuck in a world that doesn't allow you to escape.

I spent almost twenty years of my life believing I wasn't worth it. In my own selfish attempt to feel accepted, I ignored my feelings. I closed off my heart. I lost trust in myself and the outside world. Despite the opportunities in front of me, I stuck to the script of life to avoid tough transitions. Eventually, the most challenging transition in my life found me when I least expected it. I made the choice to file for divorce, knowing it would tear my world apart.

It wasn't easy, but it was a choice I had to make. Unfortunately, because I wasn't prepared to deal with the repercussions of tough choices, I numbed myself with destructive behaviors that drove me further from the actual path I needed to take. It wasn't until I was reminded of my gorgeous little daughter that I could find a way to channel my pain into something greater than myself.

If you asked me if I thought I'd ever get a divorce that would eventually lead to writing a book about life, I would have laughed. I had no confidence in my own self-worth. What changed since then? I realized the separation and alienation I sensed from others were a space I'd created myself. I moved through the world caught in a space between my two selves.

It wasn't until after my divorce that I could finally connect to my heart and see where I'd lost myself. None of us really understand how powerful our beliefs and choices are until we have no choice but to take full responsibility for our lives.

Eleanor Roosevelt said that in the long run, we shape our lives, and we shape ourselves. The process never ends until we die. The choices we make are ultimately our own responsibility.

Freedom comes from accepting full responsibility for our lives, and those who can recognize that life is earned and never given will begin to see the true power of owning their story.

The truth is, our journey in life is anything but easy. If every choice we make comes with consequences, the struggles we face reflect the choices we make. So, when you complain about your life problems, remember your problems are a direct reflection of your choices.

Shortly after my marriage ended, I wrote an article about five uncomfortable truths about my divorce. I took responsibility for reframing my situation and using it as one of the most defining moments in my life. The moment I submitted my article, I felt liberated from my suffering because I finally understood what it meant to choose and accept responsibility.

I'm not saying that the way my marriage ended was okay—not at all. But recognizing my responsibility in the relationship allowed me to see those uncomfortable truths I'd been hiding behind most of my life.

This isn't me judging your way of processing the painful transitions in your life. I know what it's like to want to do everything except the things we need most to heal.

But life doesn't work that way.

Who you are is not defined by the past events in your life. This isn't a story about how time heals all wounds. This is me telling you to pay attention to your choices because every choice has a consequence.

Those of us who realize life is earned, not given, are willing to face our biggest battles internally. We are ready to accept defeat and learn from our challenges. We want to become what we seek, so we do whatever it takes.

And it's not an easy path to live.

But what are you really doing when you live on this path? What happens when you decide to trust your choice to open your heart again for the first time? What happens when you choose to embrace the struggles and uncertainties in the new career you launch? What happens when you write that new book? The only way to find out is to choose to walk through those silver doors and surrender to the unknown. Because with that choice, you'll find that everything you need is right there in front of you.

I SEE YOU

I've poured my heart and soul out trying to create meaning
   You think you are writing words
      But really
         You are

Creating a new life
   One that gives me everything I've never had

Every tear, laugh, and frown turns into a story that
   means something
      to someone

Isn't that what we all want?

To be seen and heard
   At least, a little?

The Chase

There are so many layers behind our distracted selves. Before we can enter into a relationship with who we are underneath the clutter of everyday life, we must look at where we got lost in the chase.

I've learned a lot about who I am by sitting in silence. When I wanted to run, I sat with myself a little longer each day to connect with the parts of me I abandoned long ago. Waiting there for me was a lost boy buried below years of conditioning and the masks I wore. I thought I had built a life filled with love, happiness, and success. But I'd gotten caught up in the chase while I existed on the surface.

Today, I am finally getting comfortable with the deepest parts of my soul.

Author Jeff Brown calls this soulshaping. "To find your way, you will need courage. Lots of it. Soulshapers are artists, but they are also warriors. It is no easy feat to shape the inner world. You need the heart of a lion to overcome the odds. You need to fight for your right to the light."

Most of us have spent our entire lives putting others first. We exist on the surface. We abandon ourselves in hopes of fitting in. We coast through life until one day we wake up wondering where we even are and question everything we see.

If you feel triggered right now, it's a good sign that you have been running your entire life like I once did. I don't want this book to sit on your shelf. I want it to change your whole life by helping you recognize who you are underneath all the masks and emotional armor you wear. I want my words to help you connect with the parts of yourself you lost long ago.

These essays and poems are a reunion with the parts of you that you do not allow the world to see. The child in you that you have somehow forgotten. The you that you are afraid to be. The one you were born as before you got caught in the chase.

Allow your pain to speak. Feel where you chose one thing but wanted another. Take a deep breath, and let go of the identities you've been desperately clinging to that have kept you here on the surface.

When you can connect with these parts of yourself, you can easily see and feel where you are not, and allow yourself to come forward. Hold yourself here, so you never abandon yourself again.

Meet yourself in this moment longer

than the breath before. Need nothing

but the love for yourself; you are

worthy of this life, I am sure.

Deeper than the Surface

Searching for our "purpose" in life is one of the most demanding challenges we face as humans. Landing a dream job to make more money. Saving the money we make for retirement. Finding a healthy and stable relationship to start a family. The pressure we put on ourselves to find meaning in life leads to more uncertainty and overwhelm as our self-worth becomes attached to the achievements measured in life milestones.

From the ages of eighteen to thirty-five, I focused on hard work and having a stable life plan. From an outsider's perspective, my life had structure and purpose. I hit every major milestone I planned for at a young age. That's how life works, right? Work hard, achieve your goals, and you have your purpose.

But life is so fleeting when you are never honest with yourself.

One of the hardest lessons I learned in life came from my mentor telling me an uncomfortable truth I wasn't ready to hear: "Your life didn't change unexpectedly because of the divorce, it changed because you never trusted yourself." He was right. I came to the sobering realization that if I never trusted myself, why would the Universe, or anyone else for the matter.

I measured happiness, love, and success by my accomplishments. When life went well, my days were filled with passion and purpose. But when life didn't go according to plan, the achievements I based my self-worth on were gone, and I fell into despair. I created a life around proving my self-worth externally and paid a huge price at my most vulnerable moment.

I never shared this with anyone because I never felt good enough. I avoided my truth so adamantly that I chose addiction, depression, and heartbreak instead of facing it. And then, when my marriage was coming to an end, my lies caught up to me, and I was forced to really look at who I was and how I was impacting the people around me.

It's a common experience. We all want to believe we control our lives, yet we ignore what we feel inside. We walk through most of our lives wearing an identity shaped by our family, friends, and environment. There's an implicit code that governs how we should live our lives, and it's one that often leaves us lost and empty.

The truth of it all is that you can't find meaning in life if you aren't honest with yourself. **Perhaps our purpose in life is a lot deeper than the surface-level shit we've been taught to believe.**

Viktor Frankl said, "Ultimately, man should not ask what the meaning of his life is, but rather must recognize that it is he who is asked." I think what he means is that we find meaning in life by simply living it. Our purpose in life is not defined by what we do; it's who we are, how we feel, and an expression of how we live our lives at this very moment.

We can go through life, achieving these massive milestones and performing grand gestures, but personally, I don't think any of that matters if it doesn't reflect what we're feeling inside.

So how do you find your meaning in life? How do you know if what you're doing is making a difference?

Unfortunately, there's no easy answer. Our lives are uniquely ours, so our answers will be too. But I can tell you what I've learned: you are more capable than you believe yourself to be.

A lifetime of running has taught me that you're going to need patience, as much of it as you can find. The process of finding your true self takes time and thoughtful reflection. When you find something you enjoy that challenges you to step outside your comfort zone, it's a good sign that you're on to something deeper below the surface.

The question then becomes, *Do you have enough perseverance to figure out your passion?* Angela Duckworth, researcher and *New York Times* bestselling author, calls this *grit*. It's the internal energy needed to push past your comfort zone when life presents you with challenges and to follow through when everything is pulling you back.

Finding your purpose requires you to dig deeper than the surface, and it's a lot deeper than you've been taught to believe. Shame, fear, doubt, perfectionism, and self-destructive patterns are just a few of the obstacles you'll face as you begin your journey. While painful, if you continue to dig and work through the calling with consistent effort, you'll find something far more significant than you could have ever imagined.

I can understand wanting to run away from setbacks, failures, and the limiting beliefs that pull you back when you find something that calls you. I refused to work through these issues for most of my life, and it took me a long time to figure out why: I wasn't digging deep enough. I was willing to work hard, but I wasn't willing to do the real, deep work. Because I stopped too soon, I carved a path for myself that felt wrong. I felt lost. And rather than do any more digging into myself, I turned to addictions, depression, and divorce.

Most people I knew told me to move on in life. They told me I should use my MBA to get a salary job and stop playing around. Grow up. But I knew I was heading for something greater and didn't let their opinions influence what I was building.

Thankfully, I met some amazing humans along my journey who showed that what I had to say was worth digging deeper.

Every day I was called to write when I woke up. I didn't have to think about the end result or what I was even doing. The words took me where I needed to go. What started as a therapeutic tool became what you are reading today. My life bled out on the empty pages all over my walls as I drew outlines, verses, and words of wisdom on large Post-It Notes. Tears seeped on the pages of my journals. It didn't happen overnight. And if you talk to anyone who has built something significant in their life, you'll see the similarities within anything worth pursuing.

Most of us never get to this point. We finance our dreams with pocket change. We exist on the surface and look for someone or something to save us. The energy we need to invest in the things that matter get lost in the pursuit of happiness: a conversation here, a text message there, scrolling on social media, and engaging in relationships that save us from navigating the challenges that come with taking the time to connect more deeply with ourselves.

They all take away from who we are underneath it all.

Purpose doesn't just show up when you make default choices that don't make sense for you. No amount of money or hard work can force you to align with the purpose you feel pulled to in your heart if you're on the wrong path. You have to learn how to find meaning in the storms of life. You have to get curious about who you are underneath everything you have covered up.

The more you know who you are underneath the masks you've been conditioned to wear, the more you'll be able to navigate tough transitions. The more you have something you're willing to fight for, the more you can live an authentic life.

These are my revelations. The purpose isn't to brag, boast, or say that I'm better. I, like you, have made countless mistakes that I've repeated throughout my life. When I decided to go all-in on writing about my life experiences, the discipline and leadership skills I gained from my life turned into something greater than myself.

What did I learn from my experiences?

There are so many layers beneath our superficial selves. If you never take the time to slow down and accept who you are, you'll miss out on all the opportunities in front of you. Much of our lives are about the chase. We never give ourselves permission to go deeper and listen to what our bodies request from us. This leaves us in a perpetual state of problem-solving based on a life that happens *to* us, not *for* us.

But you can go deeper than the surface. It starts with your willingness to close your eyes and connect with the life you have been granted. To feel your two feet that have carried you through some of your darkest and most joyful days. Though tough transitions may seem like life is a stormy sea of pain and confusion, you can always come back to this place of stillness.

If you feel lost in life, come back here often. Your breath will forever be your guide. The more you are able to breathe deeply in your body, the more you can send waves of gratitude throughout your life. In this place, you will see there is no reason to keep chasing something that was never yours.

When I write in the morning, there is a deep awakening within that becomes my playground for life. I believe we all have this inside of us, but the chaos of the world doesn't give us permission to feel what we need to be free. That's why transitions can make you feel lost.

But I can promise you this: the emotional satisfaction that comes from being aligned with the truth of who you are underneath the chaos of life is a lot less taxing than chasing something or someone that will keep running.

This is my call to you: Dig deeper than the surface. Learn to face what confronts you with curiosity. Ask yourself the difficult questions. Be brave enough to claim the life you want. Seek the answers to the biggest questions that have nagged you since the beginning. Because the more you know yourself, the more you'll be able to live a life worth living. And choosing to be honest with yourself is one of the most important things you can ever do.

Get out there and recognize where you stopped paying attention to your intuition and heart. As you begin to peel back the layers of what has been hiding beneath the surface, you'll start to see that your best work is about to begin.

Out there, people are searching for

something they will never see. I wonder

how their hearts would feel if they took

a few moments to sit with themselves and breathe.

Don't Be a Statistic

My high school English teacher, Mr. Wayne Sanderson, was one of the calmest men I'd ever met in my life.

Mr. Sanderson was that teacher everyone went to about their problems. On any given day, if you asked him for help, he would go out of his way to make you feel like you were on the right path in life. This guy had quotes from ancient philosophers like Seneca, Marcus Aurelius, and many others. There was nothing he wouldn't do to help young teenagers through their various struggles.

One day, I approached Mr. Sanderson after I decided to join the Marines, and asked him why he was always so calm and if he had any advice for a lost young man.

He paused and said these words in return: "Don't be a statistic." I looked at him in confusion, unable to grasp the concept.

He'd seen a pattern among high school students and knew that the only way to live was to embrace every moment of the process. When I sat down for evening detention, he drew a timeline with the word LIFE in capital letters above the line.

He then proceeded to say, "Your entire life will be a series of statistics. From the moment you are old enough to learn in school, you begin to develop a sense of wanting more. As you grow into a young adult, like you are, the pressure is on to excel and do more with life. And so here you are finding ways to graduate high school so you can serve."

I leaned in as he drew little stick figures and arrows around the timeline.

He continued: "When you serve, the cycle will start again as you find ways to become a leader and climb the ranks. Before you realize it, your time has ended in the service, and you'll be on another path struggling to find out who you are as you fly through life. And maybe after that, you'll start a family, see your kids grow, and realize that perhaps you've been cheated a bit to believe there is a magic formula—but the world will force you to be a statistic unless you understand that the end is death, and this, right now my young man, is life."

Like many young teenagers, I shrugged it off and went on for most of my life being a statistic. And eventually, it really hit me that being another number in the world was no longer an option.

As I unpacked boxes from my old life to start my new life, I found my senior yearbook with Mr. Sanderson's quote: "Don't be a statistic."

I finally understood what Mr. Sanderson meant when he drew on that chalkboard when I was a naive teenager twenty years ago.

For most of us, we are always living somewhere we are not. It's as if we are living, breathing statistics lost in a world of numbers somewhere. As we look for ways to fit in, we sacrifice our own needs and wants, ignore our feelings, and close off our hearts. To honor ourselves would be a form of self-expression and authenticity. Which means we would threaten the tribe, so we become another statistic in the formula of life.

I may not find a teacher like Mr. Sanderson again, but I'll never forget his words and his impact on my life. As I watch my daughter grow, I can put myself in positions that require me to flow with her life rather than force her to be a statistic in the world.

At first, I struggled with parenting as a single dad. The mornings were crazy. Bedtime routines were challenging. And transition day between households caused a lot of resistance with getting ready for school. But as we grow together, I'm reminded that the things I say and do with her right now will shape her view of the world.

I'm willing to bet you can recall painful events from your parents while growing up. Things like passive-aggressive comments and gestures you've never thought of till now. These are what I look for the most in myself.

I know my words and actions will shape my daughter's sense of self-worth and how she perceives the world for the rest of her life. It's not easy. I still get frustrated from time to time. But I find myself caring less about what she wants to wear in the morning, and I try to get on her level when she's struggling. Because I know my job as a father is to create space for her to find her authentic self.

While I want her to have goals and strive for excellence, I hope she sees too that there's no use in planning for a future that makes her unhappy because she's only focused on the destination.

The more I live life through her eyes, the less I care about numbers, and the less I need to feel like I have somewhere to go.

So how do you prevent yourself from being a statistic? How do you live fully now, instead of being another number?

The first step is always to recognize the true voice inside yourself. It won't be natural, at first, to listen to and trust that voice. But the more you do it, the stronger the habit becomes. I'd be lying to you if I said I had life all figured out. But I can tell you that as I write this book at one of the lowest points in my life, I'm enjoying the struggle, the process, and embracing uncertainty. While I have an end goal, a bigger picture in life, I will not be another statistic chasing life anymore.

The challenge then becomes to take a step back and reflect as we go through life. To pause, slow down, and realize we are not statistics.

Mr. Sanderson was right. Focusing on the next big thing will lead you to a life filled with emptiness. Without intention, the choices you make are dictated by what you're supposed to be or what others before you have been. One day, you'll wake up unrecognizable to yourself. The moment you realize you've turned into someone you never wanted to be is a complete mindfuck.

Life is messy. We're taught implicit and explicit messages of how we need to live our lives. But the truth is, like Mr. Sanderson said over twenty years ago, the next milestone in life does not matter. We can't get caught up in the chase. We must stay focused on everything happening right now.

Stop chasing. Learn how to embrace every single moment of your life. Give yourself permission to learn new formulas in life without judgment or shame. Because when you find out how to enjoy the things you have while you can, *magic* fucking happens.

Shifting my perspective has freed me from the limitations and expectations of what others think of me and has given me an authentic expression of my greatest gifts. Don't be a statistic. Be everything you are right now, while you still can take a breath.

Rejection

When I was a young Marine, I had the honor of guarding American embassies overseas for three years. I felt like James Bond.

Training with the FBI in Quantico, top-secret clearances, Third World countries, working with diplomatic officials, and armed with the latest weaponry, you could say I got the chance to play a real-life superhero.

My road to becoming a Marine Security Guard wasn't an easy path. My first few years as a Marine included a lot of personal hurdles I had to clear. My desire to be part of something greater than myself wasn't innate or authentic. Instead, I was following a set of rules I'd created in my head as a child: become part of the world's most elite fighting force. Give people a reason to think you're a success. It wasn't authentic, and I didn't always feel passionate about what I was doing.

The Marine Corps believes in a different set of rules than the ones we're given as civilians. There's an expectation to excel, and it has nothing to do with validation or acceptance. If you want to be a Marine, you earn the right to put on the uniform through hard work and dedication. This belief becomes the bedrock of Marine Corps experiences and the identity of a Marine.

Much of the first few years of a Marine's career are structured so you become proficient at your specialty and learn Marine Corps leadership fundamentals. Promotions are based on proficiency in your skills and your conduct of being a Marine. As an air traffic controller, that meant I had to focus on earning predetermined qualifications that proved mastery of the trade. Once I had those, then I could master my body. I hated that. All I cared about was pushing my body to extremes. All my leaders could see my physical progress, and I thought that would be enough to earn the promotions I thought I deserved.

I was a few days from a significant milestone in my proficiency qualifications, but based on my actions, you wouldn't be able to tell. I shrugged off any preparation as if these tests didn't actually matter. It was clear to me that I was in better shape than most Marines of my rank, so I felt like it would be a good idea to keep working on my physical fitness, ignoring my assignments as an air traffic controller. Instead, I'd just do my best to qualify for guarding American embassies.

Quick progress in my physical fitness did great things for my ego and confidence. I could knock out twenty pullups, no problem, and run three miles under twenty-one minutes. I was physically prepared for anything. Unfortunately, when you are a young Marine, none of that matters if you don't receive orders well. And I didn't. In the face of orders, I reverted to the same stubborn teenage boy I was back home. I'd joined the Marines because I felt like I had to prove myself worthy of being a Marine. That meant more than a few problems with authority. I thought I knew better about who I was and where I was headed. I didn't need input from people who didn't know me, even if they were my leaders.

Challenging the rules and the structure of the Marines is not a great plan, especially if you're new, but I couldn't help it. That's who I was. And right or wrong, the leaders had to make an example out of me to maintain order and the integrity of the ranks.

From carrying ten-gallon water jugs with bloodied hands up and down the tower stairs for hours on end to endless jumping jacks in a hurricane, I saw just about every way you can haze a young Marine. But it didn't work. I continued to push my body every day to fortify my mind.

So, here I was at twenty years old, feeling like I was ready to take on the world. They tried to break me, and I showed them it was impossible. I felt in charge of where I was headed, and there was nothing anyone could do to stop me. All I needed to do was pass my test, and I would be off to guard embassies and travel the world.

As I sat down to take my qualification test, I froze like a deer in headlights. I cracked under the pressure and couldn't speak to the aircraft coming in for landing. The test caught me off guard because I didn't study everything I needed to pass. My instructor kicked me off position, and I observed everything I worked hard for crumble in front of me.

Not only would I not qualify for embassy duty, but I also wouldn't get promoted. I had my sights focused on everything except the standards and behaviors the Marines required to get what I wanted. I felt worthless. I felt like a failure.

That day, the Marine Corps let me take the punch to the face. **And the most important thing I learned was that rejection is the Universe's way of not allowing mediocrity into our lives. It's a way to connect with deeper parts of ourselves so we don't settle for something less than what we are worth.**

Life is going to give you all sorts of mundane or pointless tasks. Your gut instinct, the one you've learned based on your fears of rejection, is to ignore them. You'll want to pass them by for more "important" tasks that prove to other people that you, too, are important. Resist that urge. Your ability to do the things that sometimes seem mundane and pointless is what will set you apart. It is your chance to foster a deeper understanding of the underrated skills that lead to a lifetime of success.

Prepare for anything by doing everything you can and everything you're asked to do. You never know what the path to your truest self will require of you. If you don't foster every skill you can, you might be shut out from the opportunities to get where you want to go. None of us enjoy rejection, especially when it threatens our identity. We want to feel accepted and validated, and we do everything we can to protect that identity. So, dedicate yourself to the mundane. Assume nothing is pointless and everything is a chance to propel you closer to who you're supposed to be.

A lot of this fear comes from things we learned growing up. We tend to personalize rejection and give it meaning before we have a chance to accept it and move forward with dignity. Ironically, choosing to pass up on slowing down and coming up with ways to improve ourselves when things don't go our way only makes us live in a state of perpetual rejection.

Getting rejected for the first time in my life gave me valuable insight into what I needed to do to be a well-rounded Marine. Thankfully, I had a mentor, Craig Clapp, who took me under his wing. I thought I'd be hazed again and ridiculed for trying to be a smart-ass. Instead, Craig challenged me to lead a small group of Marines for physical training while he trained me in the different proficiencies of air traffic control.

When I trained with him, I saw consistency in everything he did. He wasn't afraid to take a step back when needed and hammer the basics. Craig never went out of his way to prove anyone wrong, and he was one of the best leaders I've ever known. When I had the chance to lead Marines in physical training, I had a model to follow. I saw someone leading because they wanted to, because it aligned with who they were. I saw what I wanted to be. After seeing what was possible, I used my training sessions to garner a sense of pride and purpose. It helped me develop the confidence I needed to move through the hurdles I'd face. Craig taught me the importance of rejection and how to take responsibility for my life.

There will always be someone who works harder than you. There will be couples who are in better relationships. There will always be that person who is more attractive than you. There will be people you encounter who have more money. These are all inevitable facts of life.

Ultimately, the only way to navigate tough life transitions is to get comfortable with rejection by honoring what you value. If you take a step back and see rejection as an invitation, the things that challenge you will transform into opportunities for you to learn more about who you are and what you need to do to become what you seek.

The more we lean into rejection, the less we care about the outcome. Rejection no longer feels like a dead-end, but rather, an invitation to explore a new route, one that is more aligned with who we are and what we care about. We begin to develop a sense of meaning when we prioritize our own values. I did not like air traffic control. But I could focus on the fact that I chose to become a Marine. I was the only one who could adapt to get what I wanted.

When we approach rejection with an open mind, we are more empowered to go after the things we want in life. I'm not going to promise rejection won't hurt because it will most certainly sting, especially when you least expect it. But sometimes we have to be honest with ourselves and ask if we are truly doing all we can to get what we want.

In hindsight, I probably wouldn't have qualified for Marine Security Guard at such a young age and rank because there were strict requirements. I thought other Marines were lazy because they liked air traffic control and were average in physical fitness. Ironically, this harsh judgment was merely a reflection of something I wanted but did not have.

In the end, I didn't let rejection get the best of me. I learned a lot about mastering leadership basics and found out more about who I was as a young man. And within three months, I completed my air traffic control requirements and was one of the youngest Marines to get accepted to guard embassies.

Rejection is a life skill that has provided me with more opportunities than I could have ever imagined. It also happens to be how I wrote this book. Everything I initially considered a failure became an invitation to dive inward and keep moving forward.

The point is this: you can make excuses to justify why something has not or will not work out, or you can accept rejection as an invitation to go deeper within yourself. Ditch the idea that you can control life. Rejection is often needed to learn how to step toward the future you truly want to create. May we learn to accept rejection as an invitation to a new life waiting for us.

You Gotta Believe
In Yourself First

The first time I sat down to rewrite this book and shape it into the words you're reading, I stumbled upon a beautiful expression in Sanskrit: "Tat tvam asi," which means "You are that" or "That you are." I was searching for a higher purpose in life and needed something to believe in greater than myself.

As it turns out, a twelve-year-old boy around the sixth century BCE was looking for the same thing. After studying and seeking the meaning in life for twelve years, he returned home to his father as a proud twenty-four-year-old young man eager to share his expertise and knowledge as if he'd figured out the meaning in life.

When his father saw his son's attitude, he asked him, "O my son! Have you studied that thing knowing which everything becomes known?" The young man was puzzled. He realized he still had not learned the Universe's essential things, and with humility, requested his father teach him the essential thing in which everything else becomes known.

After the father taught his son about the way of life, he concluded with the statement, "Tat tvam asi," one of the most known phrases in the Sanskrit language. That is to say—we are all connected, we are what we seek, and we are a reflection of what we see and believe to be true.

The urge to find meaning in life is universal. If anything, I have come to understand that much of what we seek directly correlates with our beliefs. Many of those beliefs come from an outdated system that forces us to believe and see only part of the equation. We walk through our lives watching, surveying, and observing every event through the viewpoint of others. Some of what we seek and believe is true, but many of us will focus only on the things we want to see. We ignore the details that are too painful, or inconsistent with who we want to think we are.

Do you remember being a kid, when time would fly by? You spent hours on anything you were interested in, as if nothing else mattered in the world? You made decisions based on the most fun or interesting thing in that moment. Nothing had meaning if it wasn't important to you. It didn't matter if you laughed, cried, or got into some trouble, you believed in exploring and the joy that came from figuring things out.

Somewhere along the way, we lost that childlike wonder. As we grew up, the unconscious mind created rules and narratives around what things meant based on our experiences. As such, things weren't fun anymore, and then suddenly, a lot more mattered. Now, an hour spent imagining new possibilities or bizarre scenarios isn't a creative activity; it's a waste of time. It's time you could have spent making money, networking, or pushing yourself toward the next accomplishment. Now, if you're not producing, you're wasting time.

Like right now, you're probably searching for keywords and phrases to find a way to relate my story to your life and reject what isn't useful. Psychologists call these thoughts "cognitive biases," and these biases are good at telling you to believe and see the world through a one-sided lens.

Not all of these biases are bad. Biologically, cognitive biases are ingrained in our minds to keep us safe. Unfortunately, many of us end up creating stories in our minds based on our life experiences, and we tend to believe and see what we think to be true without ever taking a moment to challenge the story.

That's why so many of us have a midlife crisis. It sounds confrontational, but until we are aware of and understand the outdated beliefs we carry, most of us will keep choosing a life based on validation and expectations without ever knowing what truly makes us happy.

I bought into this concept for nearly half my life. From the moment I left the Marines, I experienced relentless and ever-increasing stress from decades of upholding an identity that no one seemed to care about except me. To avoid the parts of me that felt shameful and unworthy, I went to great extremes in the pursuit of happiness, love, fame, and success.

I completed ten years of honorable service, and I should have been grateful for what I had, especially when all of what I wanted was right there in front of me, but that didn't happen because I felt uncertain about who I was.

It started with graduate school. I only chose that path because I thought it's what a twenty-seven-year-old Marine should do. I was accepted for jobs with the FBI, FAA, and consulting firms. And I still believed I was never worthy enough.

Because I had no sense of trust within myself, I built a wall around myself with an exceptional work ethic and started a personal training career. The time I spent transforming hundreds of lives gave me a false sense of worth, but it came at a cost. Twelve-hour workdays consumed me, and I never saw my family. I was exhausted, underpaid, and running around like a headless human trying to hold it all together.

In my uncertainty, everything felt like a grind. My health slowly declined as I got sick a lot, and focus felt impossible. I wasn't even aware of what I was doing until life hit me across the head with a cosmic 2x4.

I spent so much time chasing, I lost who I was. I developed an internal belief system that my own decisions and desires didn't matter, and I lived hidden lies without observing what I felt. I believed I still wasn't worthy, and I not only hurt myself but shut out anyone who tried to help me.

If you find yourself at a place in life where you are experiencing perpetual patterns from trying to hold your life together, there is a good chance that parts of you don't believe what is possible for your life.

While it's a difficult pill to swallow, it's often the price many of us pay. We don't believe in ourselves, so we end up in unhealthy relationships, neglect our bodies, work a job that stresses us out to the max, and walk a dark path of harmful coping mechanisms to cover up the deep-rooted beliefs we have about ourselves. These deep-rooted beliefs we're afraid to express force us to believe we have no other choice in life. We often negotiate too much, and in that process of negotiation, we end up losing ourselves. It's a slow burn until we wake up and realize we have nothing left to give, and life presents us with an unexpected transition.

But what if you could, if only for this moment, stop searching?

What would it feel like to connect with parts of you that feel lost?

How would your life be different if you accepted all of who you were rather than run?

It takes immense courage and strength to choose this place of reflection. Notice what you feel in this nonjudgmental space. Your breath and this feeling of wholeness is your essence. Even after all the hardships you've been through, or will go through, you can always come back to yourself here in the quiet moments of your breath.

I'll never judge or disrespect anyone going through a tough life transition. Nor will I promise you that sitting around wishing for something better will change your life because life doesn't work that way. No matter how hard you try to fight it, life will continuously remind you to align with what you believe and who you are. **We are defined by what we choose, and beliefs are a direct correlation to our lives.** So if you don't believe in yourself and what is possible, you will never be able to lean into what the Universe has to offer.

Learning how to change your beliefs will suck. When you discover the outdated beliefs forcing you to be someone you're not, you may encounter resistance from everyone around you, and you might even feel alone in the process, but that's okay; eventually, you will become more comfortable. And you'll wonder why you didn't start your true journey earlier.

How you choose to respond in this moment

is woven into the fabric of your life.

The pain you feel and your relationship to

change all come with a price.

Illusions

The discomfort you feel is

an illusion in your mind.

The sense you are not enough is

a part of you that you must find.

In this life, I have accepted I am nothing but an illusion. Even as I write these words, I can get lost in the knowledge that my thoughts are a series of experiences that make me feel connected to something greater. As I float between worlds of creativity and darkness, I often can't arrive at a single conclusion of who I am. The answers we seek to heal our hearts and souls are nothing but an image of the mind. The truth is, we're all on an endless journey into the unknown.

The world told me at eighteen it was time to grow up and be a man. I ran away to the Marine Corps, detached myself from everyone and anyone who tried to get close, and became another statistic. As a result, I never felt worthy, and chased all the wrong things to fill the void.

Lost in a sea of stress about yesterday and worries for tomorrow, I drowned from constant self-doubt. Then, one day, writing offered me a life raft. It helped me dig a bit deeper into the drivers in my life. Writing started to reveal the patterns that kept me stuck in a meaningless lifestyle. I saw how my existing on the surface was not healing my pain but recycling the hurt. With this new perspective, I began my initiation into unknown territory. I found ways to believe in myself a bit more each day.

A good friend asked me, "Why do you continue to believe those things about your life? Why do you put yourself through this torture? Fuck that, man."

I paused in silence. I knew he was right. So many of us live on the surface, guided by a set of beliefs designed to keep us lost. Sometimes those beliefs protect us, but most of what we believe is merely a coverup for the deep-rooted fears we're afraid to face.

I was my greatest opponent on the windy road to nowhere, facing struggles that were a reflection of my beliefs. These are the words I wrote in my journal one morning after a meditation session while tears came down my face:

*Hiding behind shame, fear, and limiting
beliefs with a heavy heart.*

Inside and outside, I watch my world fall apart.

I cried a lot after I got sober. Those early days of sobriety taught me to slow down and see that there was nowhere to go. It was painful to dive inward and open my heart. As I merged with parts of me that no longer existed, I wanted to run far away where no one knew who I was or what I'd done. But something called me to meditate and write every morning. I felt my heart scream at me in silence, telling me to forgive myself. Telling me I am worthy of love, and of being chosen.

Growing up, having my own voice in life felt impossible. When I wanted to speak, no one was around to listen. Betrayal, heartbreak, pain, and frustration. Protection mechanisms stamped on my heart from the last generation. Caught in the chase, believing that if I could achieve more in life, I'd be okay. But I never was. It was all an illusion.

I left parts of me behind many years ago in search of something to fill what I thought was lacking. One day I was living the dream, the next day I was in a bottomless pit of despair dancing with death himself. Mistakes were made. Hearts were broken. Harsh lessons became a story I was called to write. The heaviness I'd felt my entire life was a reflection of the beliefs I had for myself.

It's hard to believe in yourself when your entire life was created by beliefs that don't serve you today. Anger, resentment, and negative beliefs forced me to hide on the surface for many years. But today, I know that's nothing more than a bullshit story I fed myself.

My divorce and everything that followed was a hidden gift because it forced me to question everything about life.

As my heart shattered into a million pieces, I realized I was trapped somewhere between the past and future, watching my life drift apart. Feeling shameful over what happened, I had more resentment for myself than for anyone else. All those things I wanted to be true about life were no longer true.

All I wanted to do was hold on to the emotional armor that had kept me going my entire life. But the wounds were too deep, and I couldn't hold on anymore. It was time to take off my armor and stop this cycle of running by giving myself permission to slow down and feel. Quite possibly for the first time ever.

Living on the surface wouldn't heal my heart. Being another statistic wouldn't help me honor my authentic self. Not believing in myself wouldn't help raise my daughter.

Chasing life almost killed me. I thought I'd outrun my past, but instead it consumed everything I was.

As a result, I now question things I hear, see, and read because I believe the key to the freedom in my life comes from watching the world adjust to my beliefs and values rather than losing myself in the process. Everything is eligible for questioning and examination. Nothing is sacred. We live in a world that encourages us to run from the joyous times in life by filling them with negatives. Our beliefs about life make us forfeit our individualism so society at large can feel more comfortable.

Before you get lost on the surface and become another number in a relentless world, ask yourself, **"Is what I'm doing with my life serving who I want to become and what I believe inside?"** If your answer doesn't question your way of living, then chances are it's time for you to dig deeper below the surface so you can find what you are capable of becoming.

You can't settle for life.
Things will never be fine if you
believe they can be great.

Your heart will always be calling you to
something greater if you settle.

Take the leap to open your heart, because
it knows what you really want.

This path you are choosing will never be easy.

But it is worth it. You are worth it.

HEADLESS HUMAN

When I feel lost, empty, or hopeless these days,
  I say to myself:

Feel your way into this beautiful gift life has given to you.

Do not run again.

At the heart of your repressed emotions is the human
  experience many are not willing to face.

Welcome home.

The Storm

As hard as it is to admit, most of the transitions we face in our lives provide us with an intimate experience of who we are underneath the noise and clutter of everyday life.

Caroline Myss, a *New York Times* bestselling author and internationally renowned speaker in the fields of human consciousness and spirituality, said it best when it comes to moving through difficult times in life: "Just let go. Let go of how you thought your life should be, and embrace the life that is trying to work its way into your consciousness."

I think transitions in our lives are the Universe's way of answering our calls, but not as we might have intended. In my case, I had turned away from what I was feeling. I clung to an identity that did not serve who I was behind the masks I wore.

I carried a lot of shame around my imperfections.

As a result of observing the world through a black-and-white lens, I created walls around my heart to prevent people from seeing the real George. Of course, I didn't know I was doing this at the time because I seemed to be a disciplined success story. I thought that's what high performers did. But all it gave me was a negative sense of self-worth.

In the years following my time as a Marine, I based my self-worth on performance, achievements, and material things. I carried a shield of shame and fear around my heart. As a result, my heart grew heavy, and I missed out on what were supposed to be the happiest days of a man's life. Not physically, but spiritually, I was a lost soul.

Hearts broke. I broke. Parts of me got buried deeper beneath a false identity to conform to the world's expectations of what I thought a man was supposed to be.

I never shared these feelings with anyone because I didn't want people to think I wasn't strong enough to survive. I didn't want to be viewed as a failure.

The outcome was that I never felt like I was enough. I never allowed love into my heart. Depression and divorce were the fuel for the giant tornado that collected more pain until it took everything I had.

So, in a fucked-up way, the Universe came to my calling by showing me how disconnected I was from myself and the realities unfolding around me.

At the height of my storm, I had no choice but to step into the eye. It was both painful and freeing to see what was waiting there for me—authentic self-expression. And while it took a year of fighting with the storm, I finally learned to let go of everything. As a result, I realized that I was a lot stronger than I had allowed myself to be.

If you find yourself running from the storm, I challenge you to step into the eye of what you're running from. Because only then will you be able to break free from the past.

Give yourself permission to be all of who you are.

In this moment, drop out of your head and into your heart.

All that aches right now can be transformed
into the freedoms you seek.

The truth that runs deeper than time is there
is nowhere to go, no place to be.

The Universe Doesn't Give a Fuck About Your Life

I know this title may piss some people off, but let's be honest, we don't need any more positive mantras about how the Universe has a plan for us. Generally speaking, life isn't that trustworthy. Most of life for the majority of people is about suffering. And we're good at hiding behind the superficial layers of life to disguise the pain we feel.

By the time we graduate high school, every decision we make has the potential to leave lasting consequences. Suddenly, no decision is easy or spontaneous, because everything seems to matter so much. But even with thoughtful, measured choices, we still feel out of control. As we climb the mountain of life, nothing is ever as it seems. The peaks and valleys created by our choices are rarely ones we predict or prepare for. Rather than allow this unpredictable force to give us the freedom to stop being so careful, we retreat. We double down on who we think we need to become and lose trust in our own ability to make decisions and handle the peaks and valleys of our own life. We'd rather follow the path laid out for us, because at least it's convenient. It won't be our fault if something goes wrong; we were just following the plan, following everyone else's example.

Everyone wants to feel like they belong to something. We're coded for survival, so we seek others to make our lives easier. The problem arises when we lean too much on others for our own survival. What was once meant to be a relationship that makes life more enjoyable becomes an essential, like water. We forgo our own needs or personal desires to ensure that we won't be abandoned by this other person. We keep running because validation and acceptance flow freely. Eventually, repressing our own truth becomes impossible. Innately, we recognize something is missing, so we search for anything that can save us. More relationships, more alcohol, more mind-numbing television. We'd rather choose the bad habits that are acceptable to the group rather than choose what is right for us.

That's why many of us often struggle to find a sense of self, why women still feel as if their voices don't matter, and men slave away in jobs they hate just to return home to their families as an empty soul. The patriarchal model forced us to abandon ourselves before we ever had a chance to explore who we truly were. Outdated and in desperate need of change, it's a broken paradigm promoted through social media, family values, politics, and gender/racial roles.

As a result, we continue to abandon and deny ourselves. We let our fears kick in. We hide behind masks. In the process, things break. We break. As parts of us get left behind, we continue to take on new identities to conform and meet others' expectations and needs. In our attempt to feel accepted, we ignore our feelings. We close off our hearts, and we lose trust in ourselves.

The faces of change often come when we least expect them.

I had no clue that depression and divorce would be the most transformational moments in my life. Turns out, the Universe had a plan for me, but it was not what I intended.

As I walked through life with no emotional armor during my divorce, I felt the pain of self-abandonment. I felt the depth of my heart release the chains of my past. In this painful space, I realized I was no longer a slave to the identities that held me hostage all those years.

My struggle woke me up to the idea that at the height of the human experience is the wonderful creation of art, that what I'm experiencing might well be the answer to someone else's prayers. So, I began exploring life beyond the pain and borders of despair.

I chose to stop running and align with my mind, body, and heart. I didn't search for something outside of myself but instead connected with every part in my body that wanted me to hide.

As I desperately tried to hold on to what was, I sat there in fear among the shattered pieces of my identity. With a heavy heart and a tired soul, somehow, I found the courage to surrender to the stillness that called me toward the darkness I was afraid to face. In this space of the unknown, I was able to accept the new life trying to unfold.

It didn't happen by wishing the pain away or by bypassing it with relationships and substances. It happened by surrendering to change, letting go of all my attachment to life, and waiting patiently for the new life that was unfolding.

On those days I felt heavy and lost, I realized the Universe wasn't going to save me. In those moments of doubt, I had to find the strength to save myself. When the world was fast asleep and I wanted to run, I found courage deep within my soul to write these words. Sure, I had the help of mentors, friends, and coaches, but I found something greater when I chose to simply just be.

There is great value in letting go of this attachment to the way we think life should be, so new dreams and life can grow during some of our darkest days.

You may have found yourself in the same position as I was in, desperately holding on to the only things you know, with a nice, scripted story. I never concerned myself with how I might write the next chapter, because I knew it would simply come to me. I would follow the story everyone else had. In some ways, it was easier that way. There are fewer pages, paragraphs, verses, and words to create. But the longer we allow our story to be written by outside forces, the longer we remain trapped. We aren't moving forward, but we aren't moving back to fix our past either. We're on a treadmill, going through the motions of living, but not actually going anywhere.

Positive mantras have sold us an idea that something will save us, and everything is part of the journey. **When we get to those tough transitions in life, we realize the Universe doesn't come to our calling when we want it to.** In fact, it could give less fucks about my life, or anyone else's, for the matter.

Naturally, when I mention "the Universe doesn't give a fuck," people are quick to judge, especially those who have experienced unforeseen amounts of abuse and trauma.

To this, I say, I'm not talking about endemic pain from war, rape, child abuse, physical abuse, or human trafficking. I'm not qualified to write on those subjects. I'm talking about those perpetual patterns in life we don't want to identify with, so we look for something or someone to save us. In this frame of mind, the Universe doesn't answer our beckon just because we want to be over the misery. Instead, it provides us with ample opportunities to wake the fuck up.

Most of the struggles we face reflect something we had a part in creating. It's as if tough transitions are the Universe's way of showing us how aligned we are with our behaviors and choices in life.

Not by magically thinking this existential force is going to save us.

We can look to all the positive mantras in the world to justify why things happen or why we aren't where we want to be. Or we can stop running and choose ourselves for the first time. In this place, we can watch the world adjust to who we are instead of constantly chasing and trying to match the world. This is the power of the Universe.

When unexpected change stares you dead in the face, I urge you to take a deep breath and look into the unknown not with fear but with curiosity and a renewed outlook for your life. In this space, the Universe will remind you that your time on earth is limited. When everything in life has been shaken the fuck up, you might just have to ask yourself, **"How badly do you want the life you say you want, and what are you willing to do for it?"**

Adi Da Samraj said, "Notice what is affecting you. In one fashion or another, through the Grace of Truth Itself, you must handle business—even after the fact, at a later date. You must. You cannot continue to grow, you cannot move on in the Way of the Heart, until you handle your business, until there is nothing left over, nothing unforgiven, nothing unspoken, nothing unthought."

That is to say, when your life is changing shape unexpectedly, you are given a chance to explore life on a deeper level. The more you know those moments in which you seek to run, the more you will see the parts of you longing to dance with the new reality trying to unfold. These are the moments our culture has desperately avoided.

For many of us, we may never know what that space is, let alone dare to step into the unknown. We continue to get lost in the notion that something will eventually save us. We seek answers in positive mantras, in platitudes, and in other lost souls. It never works. Here is the truth about discovering how to trust the unknown: You already have what it takes. You are the sign you've been looking for. And in the short amount of time we have on this earth, you existing here, at this moment, is evidence that you already have what you need deep within your heart and soul.

How do I know? I experienced it. I literally saved my own life. Alone, in that car, on the darkest day of my life, I saved myself from the me that was created by relying on something external. Of course, forces of the Universe pulled me toward saving my own life. But it was up to me to listen. I had to be open to hearing my true calling, and trusting that I could make it happen. It was incredibly difficult and took coming face- to-face with death to realize that I am what I've been searching for. That a man who can be broken and stubborn can be exactly the same man who walks out of the darkness and into truth.

The difference between the man writing this book today, and the man yesterday is that I have found trust at the heart of all my experiences. The doubts don't stop coming. I still have days when I consider taking the easy road, knowing that I could experience less pain in the moment if I just did what was expected of me. But I know now the cost is too high. Not only that, but the reward of trusting when my heart speaks to me is too great to ignore. It isn't just believing in myself that gets me to wake up every day with a fire inside; it's actually listening to myself when those feelings arise.

There's an incredible feeling we get when we learn to trust ourselves and know that our lives are always in the unknown.

When life changes unexpectedly, we must remember that we are the creators of our stories. Learning to trust life requires letting go of the parts of life we desperately try to hold on to. Suppose we can give ourselves permission to sit in all the moments in life that challenge all we think to be true without judgment and without looking for something to save us. Then the new landscape we are given becomes a place for us to grow into something greater than ourselves.

There comes a point where you must find

courage to journey into the depths

of your heart and soul.

Here is where the Universe

will show you that you are never in control.

Thousand-Yard Stare

*You are but a headless human, disconnected from yourself
and the outside world. Combat veteran and athlete.
Husband and father. MBA and coach. Who are you?*

These are the words I wrote to myself a few mornings before my
life spiraled out of control.

While I'd earned a few impressive achievements at the age of
thirty-four, none of that mattered. I felt like something or someone was alongside me. Left and abreast every step, right there
with me as I felt my life slowly falling apart. I couldn't tell why
or even what was happening, but I felt the presence of darkness
take over my life.

With whatever strength I had left, I headed to the gym for an
intense workout. That morning, after a heavy set of deadlifts, I
prayed for tears to come. But they never did. I found no solace.

As much as I tried to avoid really looking at myself, I couldn't fight it anymore, and found myself looking at the mirror.

It was the first time I found the courage to stare into the depths of my soul and see the thousand-yard stare glaring in the reflection. The man I saw had the unfocused glaze of a weathered soul detached from the world. It was as if he was questioning my entire existence. And for good reason. I was a headless human passively rushing through life. Each time I looked in the mirror over the next few months, I had no clue who the man staring back at me was.

As with most revelations, it would've been impossible for me to learn this on my own. I needed to go through the experience to realize who I am is not determined by my outcomes or achievements. I'd chased life and drowned myself in useless shit that didn't matter. I wish I could've slowed down after I left the service, but I went all in, and nothing could convince me otherwise.

That drive did more for me in life than I could've ever imagined.

A high-paying contract overseas led to traveling the world with my then-girlfriend. A 3.7 GPA in grad school landed me interviews with the FBI and some of the world's top consulting firms. A surprise engagement caught on the local news that led to a gorgeous wedding on a beach and a beautiful daughter. A four-month unpaid internship at one of the top strength and conditioning facilities in the world led to becoming a coach on their staff and eventually venturing out on my own.

Paradoxically, while I had everything I wanted, I felt disconnected and empty.

There was a hidden voice behind my perceived success. A voice that would crawl up my back on to my shoulders to feed off my insecurities. Words that forced a brutal war between my internal and external world. Every day, I would tell myself, "You will never be good enough, you are a failure, you are not worthy, it's all your fault."

Battle scars formed from my past drove me to build walls of anger, guilt, resentment, and shame. Every time I met someone who had something I didn't, I'd take an inventory of my life and wonder why I wasn't good enough. I became insecure around these people, and I'd use that feeling to measure my success.

Eventually, those insecurities caught up to me. A mentor and well-known business coach in the fitness industry saw me struggling and said, "I'm wondering if transitioning to something that is a better fit for your life changes would be the right thing for you?" but I was too stubborn to listen.

He wasn't the only person who tried to tell me to slow down. My wife tried talking to me multiple times, but all I heard was that I was never good enough for her. My insecurities got louder, and I shut her down too.

Marriage and fatherhood are supposed to be some of the happiest days of a man's life, but my insecurities found their way into everything I did. I silently beat myself up by working longer hours, binge drinking, and shutting out anyone who tried to get close to me.

I was afraid I wouldn't live up to the legacy of a Marine if I let people know I was struggling. I came up with all sorts of excuses to keep myself buried in work. I was hard on myself on every level of life, and I was also hard on others. Most people thought I was a dick. I thought it was normal.

We all have those stories in our heads that create a double standard of life based on our fears. The desire to be perfect, avoid struggle, and live with exceptionally high standards is one of those stories driven by deep-rooted beliefs that cause us to close our hearts to the world.

Neale Donald Walsch said, "It is okay to be at a place of struggle. Struggle is just another word for growth. Even the most evolved beings find themselves in a place of struggle now and then. In fact, struggle is a sure sign to them that they are expanding; it is their indication of real and important progress. The only one who doesn't struggle is the one who doesn't grow. So, if you are struggling right now, see it as a terrific sign—celebrate your struggle."

Perfectionists tend to wear shields of armor to keep out anyone who tries to point out their irrational behaviors. To me, lowering my perfect shield would mean someone might see my insecurity or the messy parts. Even worse, I might have to face who I was underneath it all.

And because I refused to lower my armor, I lived disconnected from my heart and those around me that I loved most.

There is nothing wrong with having high standards and striving for excellence in life. However, when that drive turns into judgment and unhealthy competition, it's time to examine the roots of your motivation. Are you working that hard to prove something to other people? To be better than others? Or, is it your true calling to push yourself to succeed? Can your heart remain open to possibility and to the people in your life while you work toward excellence? If not, it may be time to do some reflecting.

The voice I heard when I looked deep within myself was a combination of a lost little boy and a hardened Marine who battled for attention. When I was striving for perfection, I closed off my heart because it was too painful to accept who I was. I didn't think I was doing anything wrong; everything felt normal. I was producing, and that meant I was worthy of life.

In the end, the battle between my inner and outer worlds forced me to become someone I wasn't, and I pushed others away.

When we're disconnected from ourselves, we tend to cling to the busyness of life like shit on a shovel. We are often tortured by the inner voices of shame and vulnerability.

When I saw the thousand-yard stare in the reflection, I realized I was a headless human. I wish I could tell you that things got better overnight. Instead, it took a few more years of getting caught up in the same patterns and shutting down emotionally before I was able to recognize how disconnected I was from myself and the world.

That meant finding the courage to honor my call to rest. So, I took a trip to a retreat in Colorado to find others who would support me as I journeyed into the depths of my heart and soul for the first time. It was an unfamiliar space. I was scared, but these humans invited me to rise from the depths of despair.

My mentor said to me, "The divine cannot support a half-ass decision; get out of your head and listen to your heart."

I had no clue what she meant, but something inside me did. Every morning in Colorado, I got up early to write in my journal. To my surprise, words poured out from the depths of darkness.

The shadows of your past have called you here today.

If you could speak to them, what would you say?

When did you choose to wear such armor?

Was it the pain you held closely from your mother or father?

Tell me why anger and resentment weigh you down.

*Was it when your heart got torn to pieces and
you bled out till you drowned?*

What would it feel like to surrender to silence

and speak to the wounds you found?

The only thing left to do was to face the man in the mirror again. I'd love to tell you that I don't feel that thousand-yard stare these days, but I'd be lying to myself and you. But now, instead of accepting that as the truth about me, I use it as a sign to employ some of my healthier habits. The thousand-yard stare I see when I look at myself in the mirror now is a reminder to slow down, pause, and ask myself, "Are you disconnected or connected?" The answer tells me exactly what I need to do to align myself to my truth.

When your heart feels heavy and inspiration feels dry, do not run, but instead take a few deep breaths to slow down and surrender to what life is trying to show you. We need not be held captive by perfectionism, but instead we can recognize our heart is screaming at us to lower our impossible standards and see how many opportunities are in front of us each day we wake up.

Color-Blind

I used to be color-blind. Metaphorically speaking, shame, pain, and anger were all protection mechanisms stamped on my heart from my life experiences. As a result, I did what I needed to do to survive and saw the world in one color. My heart was always open, but I stayed closed off for years. Then, at thirty-five, my heart was shattered open. First, I got divorced, and then I got sober.

These events were catalysts to healing what was accidentally scarred and broken. They were the reason I could finally see what I'd been blind to all my years. It went like this.

I wasn't ready to be a dad, and I don't think my wife expected to be a mom at twenty-six. But no one is ever ready to be a parent; you become a parent by living it, and fatherhood hit me a lot harder than I expected.

Melina's birth was one of my happiest days, yet something inside me felt different. There was a hidden voice that grew stronger by the day. A heavy heart and lost soul were the expense of holding it all together, and the hate I had for myself grew stronger every day. The feelings of tightness suffocated all those spaces in my body, and I shut down emotionally and physically. While I did everything I could to be involved, all I could manage to do was yell at my wife and stay up all night with a screaming baby, then do it all again the next day. Our endless arguments about my ridiculous work schedule took on new meaning in our relationship.

Support for each other turned to resentment and anger, and I became someone I wasn't. I worked longer, trained harder, and hit the bottle. Some days, when we were together as a family, my anger and resentment would fade, and I felt free to be who I wanted to be. But those days were few and far between. Naturally, we'd go into a cycle of fighting, making up, and going on insane adventures together. This pattern was depressing for both of us and caused an emotional indebtedness to our relationship. Until one day, after seven years together and a two-year-old daughter, the woman I thought I was going to spend the rest of my life with wanted nothing to do with me.

It felt as if sharp blades had found their way through my impenetrable force field as I heard my wife say, "I need space." The only way I knew how to defend myself against these blades was to get wasted. That night, I drowned my shame and fear with 750 ml of Grey Goose.

Another empty bottle, a night I regret.

The smell of vodka pours from my sweat.

Trapped between the past and future, I

am walking on thin ice. One wrong

step, my life, the price.

The next week I called a therapist for the first time in my life, and my wife and I agreed to couple's therapy. The resentment, loneliness, anger, jealousy, and sadness had become part of everyday life. I didn't think it was possible to drink and function like I did. Most of my days during our divorce were longer than anything I had ever experienced. It felt like hell as I fought to hold on to everything I knew.

For every good day, there were weeks of bad ones.

The only way to make it through all the fighting and screaming was to sleep on the couch and silently drink away the pain and then get up to do it all again. Inside and outside, my world fell apart. All I could do was watch as the colors of my life turned black and white.

Up until that point, I'd faced my fair share of hardships. While some of them may have seemed impossible to overcome at the time, none of them had prepared me for this. None of them were more painful than fighting through a divorce.

Unable to see the many colors of the truths unfolding, I was blind to my wife's bids for affection and ignored the parts of me desperately calling for help. Every day I woke up and carried the heavy burdens of my life, held hostage by the pain I had inside.

On Tuesdays, we went to therapy to work on our differences. But the wounds were too deep, and we continued to grow more distant. Trapped between the future and the past, I watched the world change shape in front of my eyes.

I thought we were making progress, then during one session, my wife leaned toward me and said, "I lost respect and trust for you as a man because you were never there. Physically, yes, but emotionally you couldn't see or feel me."

I freaked out. I said things I didn't mean, and I've never found the words to apologize even to this day. I knew it was the end of our marriage, so I walked out of the therapist's office that day and never went back. A few weeks later, I moved out of the house. Seven months later, we got divorced, and I got sober. It was then that I saw the vibrant colors of life and wrote these words in my journal:

The look of the future in their eyes, but they were both too lost in a story filled with passion and lust to see the truth in front of them. It would never last.

There's convenience in seeing the world in one color. We aren't born this way; we learn it from our experiences growing up. As a result, we walk around life blind and end up setting ourselves up for unhealthy experiences throughout much of our lives. The challenge is that we usually had a part in creating the tensions we face, so instead of taking time to explore the new colors, we walk around with closed-off hearts and lost souls. It's numbing here and easy to hide.

It's also in direct conflict with our most basic need to feel seen and heard by the people we love most.

Fear, shame, judgment, and anxiety create a blockage to receiving the divine gifts the Universe has to offer. We are always being seen, and the Universe listens to the words we speak. Unfortunately, what we seek or ask for doesn't always unfold the way we'd hoped.

There are endless opportunities for growth and expansion in our lives. When life seems heavy, and all feels lost, we must remember that every choice we make or do not make comes with a consequence.

We can have good intentions but make the wrong choices. Fuck, I make wrong choices all the time, yet that's how I can follow the deep, unwavering wisdom from every choice I make. I'm able to see all the colors of life as the truth shines light on the path I choose. When we realize how difficult the life we choose is and always will be, then we can have compassion for ourselves and everyone else in our lives.

The deeper we go within ourselves, the more we can take down the walls to see the beautiful colors of life in front of us. With daily practice, our breath will be our guide, and the vulnerability we feel will show us that what we all silently seek in life is fundamentally ours to own, and no one can take that from us.

You were my soulmate and came into my life to set me free.

These words I write are the gift you gave to me.

Our love was not lost.

Choices were made.

I paid the cost.

Truths

We all enter life filled with dreams higher than the clouds.
Young, naive, and filled with love, strength, and courage,
we take on challenges that put us on many different paths.
Some of us end up on a beautiful journey filled with happiness and love, others not so much. While I'm not sure why
we choose one thing over another, I am certain that the
less we listen to our hearts, the further we drift away
from ourselves.

When I left the Marines, I felt lost in the world and was afraid of
who I was as a man. Disconnected from my heart and body from
past trauma, I walked around like a headless human for years.

I built a wall around me by shutting myself off from the depths
of my heart and soul. Before I knew it, I had no sense of purpose
and my identity slowly faded as I drowned in a sea of someone
else's dreams and false beliefs.

Despite having traveled to over forty countries and surviving two combat tours, I felt like it was my hardest battle yet. Instead of fighting for something greater than myself, I was fighting with darkness himself. Civilian life was different. Any major transition in our lives will be. But I felt like no one understood who I was, so I crafted this perfect character in a story filled with charisma, discipline, enthusiasm, willpower, and drive.

In my relationship, I was afraid of being rejected even though my wife loved me for all of who I was. This fear of abandonment was something I'd run from since childhood. Rather than communicate honestly and openly about how I felt, I shut down. Love became another check box in the journey, and I disguised intimacy with intensity while I faced an internal war like nothing I could prepare for.

Combat is terrifying. There is a common enemy, and you never know what to expect. Every day is filled with unforeseen amounts of horror and loss. But no matter what, you never feel alone because you know you have a band of brothers and sisters who would do anything for you. You complete missions that seem impossible while gaining confidence and willpower to survive tough times.

Abandonment feels like combat, but with an enemy that never goes away. You feel like a lone soldier and have no idea how long the battle will last or if it will be your last breath. Instead of fighting for something greater, you're fighting voices in your head that tell you everything is your fault, and you're a failure. Without anyone to remind me I wasn't alone, I withered away. I felt like I couldn't survive this battle, and I disappeared into the shadows with no way out.

Some call this a midlife crisis. I call it the painful truth.

George Orwell said, "We are all capable of believing things which we know to be untrue, and then, when we are finally proved wrong, impudently twisting the facts so as to show that we were right. Intellectually, it is possible to carry on this process for an indefinite time: the only check on it is that sooner or later a false belief bumps up against solid reality, usually on a battlefield."

So many of us are on the battlefield every day. Unhappy relationships, unhealthy bodies, addictions, and dead-end careers become the norm. I don't know how I got here, but maybe it started because I was caught between the worlds of two different sides of myself, both so disconnected from each other, I had no choice but to seek a path that led to a heavy heart and a severed head. Or maybe everything that happened was a blessing in disguise that led me to a more authentic calling. All I know is that picking my head back up and connecting it to my body has been one of the most painful things I've ever done.

Unexpected life changes, facing the man with the thousand-yard stare, and slowing down to notice all the vibrant colors around me gave me the strength to breathe through the pain with an open heart.

I started to think about all the ways I lost trust in myself many moons ago. I thought about the times I got stupidly drunk. The times I flipped out for no apparent reason. The times I said yes when I really wanted to say no. While painful to think about, I felt free because these memories showed me that my story was worth living. It made me understand how I got here, and that I wasn't a failure. Everything I did in my life was a reflection of a story written by someone else.

I finally choose myself first, and in this space of authenticity, I am not afraid of owning all of who I am. Now I get to be the creator of my next chapter. Here's something I wrote when I had this revelation:

I get lost in the way I let go when my words bleed

out in the form of a story. Surrendering to the

unknown takes me one step closer to my

truth. Who am I to run away from my youth?

So here I am, with my wounds bleeding out in the form of words because I believe that someone else like me might be feeling the same. In this moment of stillness, when the world is fast asleep, life itself brews a force greater than what I seek in the past or the future.

I hope that as you read my stories and poems, you'll begin to notice a difference between who you were a few pages ago and who you are at this moment. To do that, you have to accept all of who you are by finding the courage to pick up your head, connect it to your body, and choose to narrow the gap between your inner and outer worlds.

Here you will find a green pinpoint of light at the center of your heart. It's the chakra of love and is referred to in Sanskrit as the *Anahata*. No walls can withstand the compassion and self-worth that come from this place of acceptance. Breathe deep into the center of your heart to allow forgiveness into those dark areas. To let go of grievances. To be kinder to yourself. This is how you align with parts of you that were once lost. Do this every day, and you will find what your heart and soul need. Because when what was once true is no longer true in this moment, you show up in the world greater than who you were just a few breaths before.

I turned myself into a writer to ensure my life would become a reflection of my heart and soul. These words free me from my past and also allow others to heal their wounds. Words are so powerful;

they replace what the real world can't give me. I write about my heart because I discover how to become more intimate in a world full of detachment. Each verse spills over to dispel the myths associated with unworthiness and a heavy heart. It's not about creating a fairytale; it's about my quest for emotional authenticity because my words will forever speak my truth.

✒

On the days you feel heavy and lost, if you try

to move too quickly, it'll come at a cost.

Protect yourself in these moments

or your head will get severed and lost in a sea

of false beliefs. Listen to your heart's center

speak, it will give you the freedom to breathe.

Disconnected, to connected.

Life is here, not there.

REMINDERS

I am in the spaces between.

Love and betrayal.

Pain and comfort.

Chaos and control.

Clarity and disorder.

Stillness and anxiety.

Open and closed.

Acceptance and resistance.

Life and death.

Uncertainty

When I found out I was going to be a dad, my entire world stopped. It was as if Father Time himself cranked on my dial of life and gave me the one thing I needed to slow down—the life of a child.

My wife was afraid to tell me because she wasn't sure how I'd react. And to be truthful, neither did I. *I'm going to be a dad,* I thought as my body froze with fear.

I'd been chasing life for the last fifteen years. I'd destroyed my sense of self-worth. I had no clue who the man in the mirror was. We'd just gotten married. I had something else planned. The Universe had another.

Something inside me changed that day, and I couldn't recognize what it was till I wrote this section. It was the moment where I felt that maybe I could change everything. Perhaps I didn't have to end up like my parents—and then I did.

I thought of this all day long and hard while wanting to run from everything when writing this book.

Because I had a deep-rooted fear that I was never worthy enough, I developed walls that prevented me from slowing down and showing up to the world as my authentic self. I tried so hard to be a perfectionist, and I let my past influence my future. Every choice I made reflected what I saw and believed to be true about life from my childhood.

It was a sobering revelation because I saw how vulnerable I was to my past and others' opinions. It caused me a lot of pain because I showed up in the world with fear instead of love. It's not that I didn't want to love, but that I tried so hard to fix something that never needed fixing.

Fast forward five years. I'm living in my hometown as a divorced single dad. I'm sober, happier, and healthier than ever before. More importantly, I believe and know I am worthy of love and anything I desire.

There is nothing more potent in life for an invitation to grow and expand than becoming a parent. Sure, divorce taught me a lot about who I was and what I wanted, but my five-year-old daughter continues to be one of my greatest teachers in life.

I learned (although it hurts to admit this) that I built a life based on how I thought others should perceive me rather than being honest about who I was. As a result, I let others' thoughts and actions control how I showed up to life. What I've come to recognize now and accept is that we are the only person responsible for our lives.

Melina is a brave tiny human who loves me unconditionally. Every day I spend with her is a day to embrace love. Her love comes with no expectations or limitations—but only if I can embrace uncertainty and let go of how I think life needs to be.

Of course, this isn't easy, and I'm just getting comfortable with this new life in front of me. But fatherhood teaches me to connect with the parts of me that felt rejected and abandoned as a child. It allows me to see miracles happening because every day is a new day to start over again.

I sometimes struggle to slow down, to be engaged with my daughter when she wants to play and I have work to do. But I now know that within every struggle comes a cost.

I wasn't sure I was going to write this. The shame associated with seeing parts of my life repeat from childhood caused me to sit in an emotional pit of turmoil. I deleted parts of this book multiple times. Every morning I felt frustrated as I explored my feelings of incompetence and defectiveness. It took me months to stop fighting the tears that needed to come through, given how much shame I had to work with. But fatherhood gave me the courage and strength to turn inward and allow me to fully embody all of who I am. And that speaks to how powerful this essay is.

Each moment we are given another precious breath is a moment we will never get back. Sobriety in my life has awakened me to this idea that miracles happen in times of uncertainty.

Whether I doubt myself writing these words, struggle with parenting, or any other personal decision, I think to myself, *What a privilege it is to choose the struggle of being here in these moments of uncertainty.*

I slow down because I have danced with darkness himself, and that dance reminds me to feel it all. After many years of running, I'm developing a relationship with uncertainty. We are walking when I want to run.

Melina is my reminder to slow down. All I have to do is watch her engage in life and see how everything she does is about being immersed in those moments that seem mundane. Then I have to trust myself, no matter how difficult life may seem. Because the more I can connect deeper with myself and slow down, the more miracles unfold in times of uncertainty.

Every morning I remind myself to slow down by sitting in silence.

*Sometimes you need to sit silently in
the early hours of the morning.*

*With a cup of coffee and the blank pages
of a notebook, you might*

*just find your heart as you enjoy the comfort
of yourself for the first time.*

Records

One evening I found myself at a friend's house as I struggled with my divorce. I was intrigued by the massive collection of albums on her wall. Each album was meticulously organized by year and color. I asked her about her music selection while she rolled a perfectly crafted joint. She looked at me and said, "In these albums, I get lost in the experience from beginning to end, and that is a beautiful reminder for me to slow down and appreciate every detail life has to offer."

We got high while she played *Goodbye Yellow Brick Road* by Elton John. It has an eccentric cover loaded with images from what looks like the *Wizard of Oz*. As I watched her dance, she explained happiness in a way I'd never heard before: "Not only are we listening to one of the greatest albums of this time, but this album is a reminder of how good life is when we go back to our roots."

I'm not sure if it was the weed, the music, or the way she looked at me, but something about that moment made me realize that all the things I was chasing had led me to become the man I was. I accepted a million songs in my pocket and lost sight of the beautifully crafted tunes in a fast-paced, digitalized world.

Listening to that album showed me how to slow down and enjoy the moment while I looked at life through a different lens. It was an approach I hadn't considered before I heard that record play.

That record allowed me to see that our unique experiences create happiness, not the materials of a fast-paced, digitized world.

Listening to *Goodbye Yellow Brick Road* with her paid off. As I refocused my energy by slowing down, I began to write, and I began to experience happiness for what it was—the present moment. When I engage in what keeps me grounded, I see, hear, and feel all that is real, and nothing else matters.

So many of us spend our lives drowning in options. The fear of missing out on what we want leads us to remain in a constant mode of starvation—connected to ideals rather than our hearts. As a result, we keep ourselves from appreciating the more delicate tunes in life because we have so many options at our fingertips. With records, you don't have that option. From the moment you pull the album out of its sleeve, you're committed to the process. It's a ritual that reminds you how uncomplicated our lives, too, can be.

Most days, when I hear a dull sound playing in my life's background, I refer back to the day when I listened to this record. I've come to know the fast-paced hum of the world and have only recently begun to understand how to slow down when I find myself wanting to move fast. Records remind me that happiness is within every breath, word, and detail that surrounds me. Each day I am granted another precious day to live is another day I can listen to the track that is playing right now. And like a record, the more you slow down and listen, the better it sounds each time it plays.

As you read these words, consider that happiness is here in what might be a brief moment when you step outside your head and into your heart. Maybe even feel a sense of relief as you feel things you haven't felt in a long time. Remember this feeling when you seek to check out of the real world and into the digitized world. Because while it's tempting to move fast and download the millions of songs available, you always have the choice to slow down, pull out a record, and listen to every track in front of you.

Maybe if we all slowed down to listen to full albums, we'd need fewer things to make us happy. I realized my friend enjoyed life because her happiness came from being present, not getting lost in the digitized world. Whatever happiness means to you, the experiences you get from slowing down are far greater than anything that moves fast in life. When you can tune into what is here, and now, you can begin to live.

The Spaces Between

Two years ago, I went down to Florida to stay with my cousin after my wife said she needed space. I couldn't sleep and found myself by his pool in the early hours of the morning. As I looked out on the dark shadows across the dimly lit path of water in front of me, the sounds of silence called me to be still. It was an unfamiliar feeling. One that left me questioning everything about life.

I didn't know what I was doing at the time, but I decided to sit in the shallow end of the pool and take a few deep breaths. With every exhale, I could feel the falsehood of all my identities fighting to hold on. I closed my eyes, took a deep inhale, and submerged my entire body into the pool. I let go, sank deeper, and surrendered to the present moment taking shape.

The heaviness I felt from years of repressed emotions sunk me to the bottom of a pool like an unwavering anchor in a wild sea. Trapped in a battle where two realities could not coexist, the patterns of my past appeared in vivid flashbacks of death, betrayal, and pain.

I screamed as loud as I could, but no one could hear me. Darkness held me down and my body shook uncontrollably. Somehow, I found the strength to stay a little longer in the place of tension as my body released and floated back to the top of the pool.

I don't know how long I was at the bottom of the pool or how I managed to surface back to the top. It doesn't matter. What matters is I stepped beyond myself that day. I entered the unknown, surrendered to the water, and found something greater.

Lao Tzu said, "As a rule, whatever is fluid, soft, and yielding will overcome whatever is rigid and hard."

When we are in deep suffering, we often wish for the pain to go away. While these difficult moments make us want to resist life, the spaces between our internal and external worlds are reminders to connect deeper with our hearts.

For a long time, I was afraid of silence. The identities I'd created made me believe that I would somehow suffer less if I avoided sitting with myself, so I hid behind walls. But like the eternal battle between sea and shore, my walls eventually wore down. The storm that was my true self was too strong. The years I spent ignoring silence, allowed the storm to get stronger, more intense.

I'd used my time to numb myself rather than get strong enough to face the darkness, and so, when the storm came, there was nothing I could do to stop it.

Today, I am here with my wounds, as many of you are, because I know life is, and will always be, a heavy storm. In order to bridge the gap between our internal and external worlds, we must become one with the stillness we are afraid of. We must slow down and take the time to step into a more conscious and deliberate life rather than run when everything feels heavy.

Take a few moments to breathe and endeavor to open what was once closed off. Feel the rawness of everything you are. Don't run from stillness, embrace it. Because this is your life and everything you desire are qualities that will come from things buried deep within.

We tend to avoid stillness because we're afraid of what we might find, but we must remember that we are all collectively working to heal what once torn us apart. Here we will find a universal truth, that the spaces between our external and internal worlds are companions of life, and resistance to those spaces is the companion of death.

If you give yourself permission to sit in silence, you might notice feelings calling for attention, and parts of you that you left behind in search of a life worth living. Some days you will find sadness;

other days you will find relief, confusion, and detachment. But each feeling that comes and wraps itself around you is there to help you go deeper with yourself. To let your heart lead, even if it means feeling all the things many are not willing to face.

With daily practice, you will begin to see that what you seek outside yourself is fundamentally yours to own as you find the courage to step into the unknown. When you find your breath, it will hold you strong as you dig deep to connect with your heart. Remember, you always have a choice to run away from stillness, or step in between where the mystery of life shows you the truth of who you are and what you seek. Take a deep breath, put a hand on your heart, and feel your heart speak words of wisdom to remind you how much you have grown as you face the unknown.

After I got out of the pool, I felt grounded and alive. It was the first time in my life that I saw how my thoughts, beliefs, and expectations of the world caused me to experience so much pain. Waves of compassion and freedom flowed through me. My soul needed me to sink to the bottom of the pool to initiate my healing process. Unfortunately, I was caught between a past I wished didn't happen, and a future that was unfolding in a way I'd never planned.

It took me almost a year of running before I found the courage to file for divorce. When I walked into the courtroom, I remembered the quiet morning by the pool. Goosebumps ran throughout my body as two worlds collided before my eyes. Tears ran down my cheeks. I tried to fight them, but my shallow breaths froze me in time. Trust and distrust. Love and hate. Fear and doubt. I felt the shadows of my past paralyze my future. Somehow, I found strength to find one deep breath and sign the papers. My tears lasted only a few seconds and I went for a walk with my journal, and these words poured out while I sat in silence.

I felt my heart speak to me in the quiet

hours of the morning. Tell me why you

ignore me, why are you still performing?

As we discover how to trust ourselves, we can step away from our interpretations of life and transcend our judgment of the moment. We can allow ourselves to see the love shining through the darkness so long as we let our hearts speak. The spaces between are where we will find the keys to the freedom we seek and the beautiful story of life waiting to unfold. Arrive at your breath often enough, and you will watch the parts that have grown distant light up any darkness that comes your way.

It is true, the spaces between bring sadness, relief,

confusion, and detachment. But each feeling that

comes and wraps itself around you is here to

help you go deeper with yourself. To let

your heart lead, even if it means

feeling all of the things you are not willing to face.

You are in the spaces between and it costs nothing to breathe.

Release and be free.

Welcome to the spaces between.

Silent Voices

A week after my divorce, I found myself sitting lakeside with one of my best friends about to tell him how I felt.

For nearly twenty years, silent voices had played in the background of my life and suffocated the spaces within my body that needed to breathe. I don't know if the voices were there to protect me or harm me, but eventually, the voices got so loud, I had nowhere to escape.

Ralph Waldo Emerson said, "These are the voices which we hear in solitude, but they grow faint and inaudible as we enter into the world."

When I left the Marines, these voices guided me into the deep waters of the unknown. We walked together for years.

Hiding behind walls didn't require much effort from me. It meant blocking out those voices with hard training sessions, alcohol, and long workdays. When I discovered how to numb the pain, my heart closed, my soul froze in time, and the voices got quiet but never went away. I had an empty heart and a heavy soul at the expense of a false identity. People complimented me on my accomplishments, as if I was disciplined and successful. They didn't see a man desperately calling for help.

Depression is complicated, silent, and dangerous. I needed a way to survive the heaviness of feeling trapped by the overwhelming unhappiness caused by the shadows of my past, so I built an identity to silence the voices. The Marine was a noble defender, but he was also temperamental and created a disconnect between anyone who tried to get close. In this space, I seemed to function at impossibly high levels.

It would be unfair to say that everything in my life was dark. In fact, by my standards, I had everything I wanted and asked for in life. But I felt trapped somewhere between the past and future and far from the present. Happiness managed to slip away like water in cupped hands as I passively walked through life, drowning the voices.

Most nights were sleepless as I spent hours staring at the walls, thinking about the afterlife. I was exhausted, felt unseen, unheard, frozen in time, and was fucking dying inside. On the drive to work, I wondered what would happen if I ran into the guard rails. And that was just the beginning.

On more than a few occasions, I found myself on bridges in the middle of nowhere, afraid of the voices inside me, trying to decide what my life would look like without darkness following me around. I'd sit there for hours some days, staring at the water below, thinking about how my body would be an empty soul, nowhere to be found if I just jumped.

Strange as it may seem, I floated between worlds of darkness and light as I danced with death himself. It felt powerful to have that sort of control over my life. Eventually, these voices made it through my armor, and I bled out at the sight of betrayal. Not even a tourniquet could save me.

And so I found myself at the lake in New Hampshire with my best friend and nothing left to lose. We started talking about our lives over beers and nature. Most people will do everything they can to avoid uncomfortable conversations, but not Eric. He was there to listen.

As we sat by the fire, I heard these voices speak for the first time in my life. I felt awful at first but found the courage to open my heart and tell Eric how I felt. "All my life, I've been pretending to fit in. These days, I see everyone else is as fucked up as I am. I'm not okay on most days, and I haven't been in a long time. I'm still having trouble understanding if my heart is broken, open, or both. I feel like a failure and have no clue who I am. What the fuck is wrong with me?"

I realized that I'd grown distant from the heart of my repressed emotions because I felt unseen and unheard in life. When these voices wanted to speak, I labeled them as a weakness and kept them silenced. I inflicted the same pain I tried to escape. The worst part is I was doing it to myself. I thought those emotions were my enemies. They didn't deserve to be acknowledged, much less understood or cared for. I was wrong. The truth is, these voices always mattered. In fact, they are my life partners. Those feelings will follow me forever, and the only real choice I have is to listen, to make sure they're felt.

That day at the lake, I chose to purge unhealthy distractions from my life, and I was amazed at how much lighter I felt. All my internal walls came down. I saw the vibrant colors off in the sunset and could finally breathe.

In this place, I made being true to myself more important than anything else in my life. I brought the darkness into the light by writing this book and learned the only way to heal what feels heavy is to walk through the storm. And that is exactly what I did.

Since the day I gave my own feelings a voice, I've stayed sober and haven't experienced any suicidal thoughts.

Conformity forces us to block out the voices. The truth is often so simple, but we complicate it by adding our own false identities, pain, ego, addiction, or other armor. We choose silence over our inner voice because it's more comfortable. No one ever wants to explore their relationship to stillness and listen intentionally to the sounds surrounding their inner body. Afraid of the truths the voices might speak, conformity keeps us numb, and it's easy to live there. Eventually, those voices will strip us bare of our identities and reveal what we need to see and hear.

When you feel disconnected from yourself, let whatever it is within you speak without judgment because your vulnerability will break down barricades even if it hurts to pause at the moment. **Much of our suffering in life comes from the resistance to years of feelings never being allowed to surface.** Do not hide behind the shadows when the voices speak. Listen to the wisdom that needs to come through because they do not follow you to haunt you but to remind you that there is a story waiting to unfold.

These days when I find myself wanting to block out the voices, I witness a separation of my identities.

There is a Marine, a noble defender who wants to run from the pain by training hard. Then there is a writer tugging at me in the early morning hours who chooses to turn his wounds into something more purposeful than shame and regret. On the other side is a man walking through the ashes at his feet to confront what has died. And then, a father of a five-year-old daughter exploring the world with curiosity and passion.

All of them have a purpose in my life. They remind me that I'm lucky to feel so deeply because maybe we're all out here, walking in a dark, twisted world. But somehow, through our struggles, we shape a new future that creates a defining moment when pain answers the questions of life we've all been secretly asking for years.

When life feels impossible, lean in and listen to what your heart is telling you because your voice matters, and so do you.

Feelings. The discovery of myself from the inside out.

It's a weird place to be as I create between the spaces

to let it all go. Suddenly, my words form

in the shape of a mentor and I am lighter as my heart softens

and the sharpness of my pen signifies I am walking

through dark caverns untouched.

Heavy Chains

On July 26, 2019, a month after I put a gun to my own head, I recorded a voice memo for myself. I was in the middle of nowhere, sitting in my car, screaming as loud as I could. My throat ached and my lungs ached for air, but I kept screaming. My mission, however crazy it may seem now, was to yell until I was free. I needed to be free from the heavy chains of my past, and nothing else was working. I'd lost everything and I still couldn't find my path to freedom. So, I figured why the fuck not. Action is better than nothing.

For precisely six minutes and fifty-five seconds, the toxic emotions I held deep beneath my heart and soul poured out until I had nothing left to shout. I took a deep breath to align the parts that felt lost, neglected, and forgotten. As I wiped the snot and tears from my face, I found the courage to look at my reflection in the rearview mirror, and a timid boy appeared in the fogginess of my view.

I was lightheaded, dizzy, and unsure what to do. So, I kept yelling. I screamed at myself and asked what the reflection wanted from me. After moments of silence that seemed like an eternity, the boy spoke to me and said, "You left me trapped behind the shadows of our past, and I carried your chains for years, unable to set myself free. Today, you have set me free."

As I continued to cry, the reflection slowly disappeared as the fog lifted. Feeling light and free, I realized the boy appeared to remind me that my greatest strengths lie within my ability to love all of who I am. The heaviness I felt reflected the resentments and self-hatred I had for myself more than anyone who harmed me. Some experiences were simple, like giving up sports as a teenager and getting into drugs and alcohol. But the heavier ones were long chains bound together by years of things I held inside.

A few weeks later, my mentor recommended I start writing about my experiences to release the pain I was unconsciously carrying, and look for ways to challenge my current life.

Fuck feelings. Those were the words that kept appearing in front of me each morning when I got up to write. There was no way I would relive the wounds I'd desperately tried to forget. I didn't want to do it, and I knew I'd feel better if I just got up and walked away from my computer. At least, temporarily. But now, I wasn't doing things for temporary fulfillment. My calling was to think long-term, to make choices based on my bigger calling. Plus, losing your whole life in a matter of months will force you to do some serious soul searching.

At first, I did everything to avoid writing. I would trick myself into waking up early, do a few pushups to get my mind right, but never return to the work that I needed to do. The only thing I seemed to do in the morning was work out early, get my daughter ready for daycare, and head to work. One morning, in the middle of distracting myself, I saw a photo on one of my social media feeds. One of my good friends from the Marines had died by overdose unexpectedly. With nothing to do and overwhelming emotions filling my heart, I started writing. I wrote all morning. And then I did it again the next day. And the next. And the next.

My friend's unfortunate death reminded me that the feelings of hopelessness I had are real. I knew if I felt the weight of those chains, as my friend did, then there had to be thousands of others who felt the same. None of us were alone, despite the isolation we felt on a daily basis. The realization that I may have a way to connect with people who feel the pain the way I do, the way my friend did, gave me the courage to write about places I never knew existed. This place is where the superficial accomplishments that we're told create a life don't matter.

Here, there's no more wondering what comes next or fretting over what happened yesterday. All I care about is releasing the heavy chains of my life through my words. The only way to do so is to accept that the only human in control of my emotional freedom is the man in the mirror.

For most of us, forgiveness is a large order. It's hard to step back and let go of those who have harmed us, let alone look at how we might have been responsible for the wounds we created. I've forgiven many things and now understand that hurt people hurt people. Maybe not on purpose, but because emotional wounds create defensiveness and heavy chains that close off the heart.

Telling others to forgive and move on with life is not something simple to say or embrace. Pain is real, hurt runs deep. We can't simply forget they exist and hope they go away. But that's what life dictates to us, especially men. Ignoring the pain is so deep in our collective patterning that I believe guilt and shame will forever follow us around. Not until we learn to speak the truth of our pain, and genuinely forgive each other, will we be able to go beyond our chains and eliminate our emotional attachment to pain.

Any attempt to escape the chains by pretending they do not exist doesn't make them go away; it makes them heavier and heavier until we have nowhere to go. And sometimes it's a dance with death earlier than we planned.

Instead of feeling the pain, we create our own masks to hide guilt, shame, fear, abandonment, and anger. We carry self-inflicted wounds on top of the wounds caused by others. It doesn't have to be this way. We can decide whether to release the chains or carry them around while weighing others down with our path.

As crazy as it seems, my voice memo helped me align parts of me that felt lost and neglected. I whispered to myself, "Losing you many years ago left me searching for something that never existed. I realized much of my life felt empty because I separated myself from you."

I sat there and took a few deep breaths and imagined hugging this little boy. With each breath, all that felt cold now felt warm. Emptiness turned to wholeness as I stitched together the divide I'd created. In my car, no story of pain could stand between the love I had for myself.

We all feel the pain from transitions that make us want to hold on. It's easy to blame others because you can run and walk around guarded as if your heart doesn't exist. Time moves on. People move on. But your heart does not. It's guarded by the plot of your past. You're a lonely soul searching for pieces of a broken heart that can only be healed by the one thing you're afraid of most—love.

Take inventory of your feelings for a second. **What are you most afraid of happening if you move forward with an open heart? Why do you struggle with letting go of the past? Now ask:** *How* *do those feelings benefit me?* **If they didn't, you wouldn't be here right now.**

Go a bit deeper now and connect to yourself in this moment. **Where did you abandon yourself (or feel abandoned) for the first time? What could you give yourself right now that would make you feel seen and heard?**

The more pain you feel, the more you'll want to hide behind masks to protect an identity that does not serve you. If you never take time to reflect and slow down, you'll never be open to the new life trying to unfold for you.

As hard as it is to connect with this part of you, it's a sobering place to be in life when you can reflect on who you truly are underneath the surface and how you show up to the world today.

Maybe forgiveness is not in your story. That is completely fine, but empowerment comes from feeling the process entirely.

We might never see the impact forgiveness has on ourselves or others, but we can see what happens in the absence of an open heart and kindness. Time is the most precious thing we have in life. The price of freedom is to see who we are today, not yesterday or tomorrow.

I breathe deep and find forgiveness in my soul

Who am I? What is the story that will be told?

A life filled with twisted sins

Self-abandonment and hatred for myself

A battle I never could win

I did the best I could with what I knew

For anyone I hurt, I am sorry it had to be you

Clean anger fuels my open heart

I will never be free until I let go of what once tore me apart

My words form a story when the world is fast asleep

Mentors that can be a guiding hand to others like me

Another Voice

So many of us avoid the spaces between. We get lost in the chaos of the world. Fear suffocates the areas in our bodies that need to breathe, and we get weighed down by years of repressed emotions. Patterns from our past influence the world we attract, and we cling to identities and stories that do not serve us.

Holding on gives us a sense of control even if we know it keeps us in those spaces we do not want to be in. But we are not our past, and if we find ways to use all the energy we take from holding on and release it to sit with ourselves in silence and listen to our hearts speak, we will see a new life standing there in front of us.

When I finally forgave myself for the first time, I recognized how I wanted to feel was far more important than the fear I was never worthy of life. I had to be mindful of the life I was choosing. That meant looking at my values. It meant I had to keep a reminder of the truths I didn't want to face. Divorce, depression, and addiction were a reflection of what I was afraid to feel. So every day after my separation, I asked myself who I was and what I was feeling. With those questions in front of me, I was able to change my unhealthy coping mechanisms into a life that contributed to something far greater than I could have ever imagined.

To surrender is such a beautiful gift. It's a word that reminds us how powerful our hearts and minds can be. Death, heartbreak, and hardships are disguises to wake us up to the patterns that no longer serve us. I have fought long and hard to learn that the wars we face always start within. They can spread up through our bodies like a web of hate and consume any chance of living with an open heart. Our only defense is to let go of all that is meant to be free, including ourselves.

Many of us will do whatever we can to hang on to our old lives because of a future that seems uncertain. The more we hold on, the heavier we become. What may seem like control is the opposite. The more we fill our lives with extras, the more vulnerable we become to the chaos of change. We assign bigger meaning to the cars we own, our social media feeds, we assume we can't make it through the night without our routine drink or other coping mechanism. It feels like control, until you lose it all. Then you're left with only yourself, and a bigger void than before. This isn't the path to freedom. We'll never be free if we continue to hold on to things, hoping to maintain control over everything.

Rumi, the famous Persian poet, said, "Try not to resist the changes that come your way. Instead let life live through you. And do not worry that your life is turning upside down. How do you know that the side you are used to is better than the one to come?"

To me, he's telling us that if we can come to a place in our lives where we are willing to surrender to the challenges we face, no matter how painful and unexpected they may be, embracing the unknown can lead to a better story.

This is the road to the other side of your tough transition. It will not be easy. It will require you to dive deeper between the spaces.

Within all of us lives another voice—one calling us to break free from the chains that weigh us down. It's a voice that shows us that we are worthy of the life we want to live. It's a voice that gives us the courage to trust ourselves in the unknown.

Even if, for one breath, you can surrender and be with the current moment, you'll hear this voice calling you to the freedom you seek. If you keep listening, you'll see that all your fears are stories you tell yourself about something that doesn't exist because you haven't trusted yourself enough to enter the unknown.

Each time you feel the dark shadows of your past call you, the breath is where you will meet yourself at the outer edges of the universe. Here, you'll find the courage to step into the unknown. Answer this call. Take the leap. I promise you, this work is a gift, and all those fears you have of surrendering are old stories waiting to be rewritten.

SHIELDS

With your heart as your guide and your feet
firmly planted on the ground

You can step inside the chaos of your life,
and hear the silent sound

Disconnected from the painful truths you
must discover how to feel

Your breath exposes a level of tenderness you have
been fighting to protect with a shield

Allow yourself to step into this space of the unknown

Your heart speaks words of wisdom to remind
you how much you've grown

You may feel lost, but your heart has never lost you

Dive deeper into the tenderness to see your truth

Vulnerability is key to the freedom you seek

Breathe deep

Lower your shield

Surrender and release

Armor

I never meant to lose myself. Despite my heart screaming at me underneath the wounds I carried, I continued to collect checked boxes in my life. I did what so many others do. I ignored what my heart said. My fear of rejection morphed into a false hero. A brave Marine who found addiction and darkness to fuel his pain. I ran from my heart for almost twenty years.

I was afraid of what was inside me because I never felt like I had a voice. It felt powerful enough to change the world. It also felt powerful enough to push me toward the end of my life.

Everything will all work out, I told myself. *I'll keep my feelings to myself because this is what a man does. I'll fake it till I make it.* But that was far from the truth.

Sometimes I wondered if I was the only human who felt this way. Maybe it's because we've all been dishonest with ourselves, trying to be someone we aren't.

People told me I had an exciting life, that I was going places and would change the world. I shrugged it off and found myself with another drink, a woman I cared nothing about, alone, empty, and exhausted from running.

I took my shield off the day I got sober. For the first time, I felt the love I'd lost for myself and the life I wanted to create. For the first time, I let my heart speak, and I actually listened.

I can feel your pain and see the heaviness
of defeat on your face.

Change is a natural part of life you must learn to embrace.

For as long as I can remember, I never spoke my truth. I never paid attention to how I showed up to the world or how I felt. I resisted change. But when everything in my life became too heavy, my shield lowered, and the only thing I could do was feel everything I was running from.

Sobriety forces me to feel the pain every day. I walk into battle with only the armor I need. When I'm not strong enough to move forward, life reminds me to choose myself. Then I feel it all because every breath I take, I will never get back.

So how do you know if you're walking around with shields? If you have to think about these words, chances are you already know the answer to what you seek.

Losing everything taught me to see the real me underneath it all. The beauty that grows from tough transitions comes from letting go. In the unknown with an open heart is how you will find yourself.

I still struggle to live with an open heart. But I have learned that within the struggle lies the power of choice. And I choose to listen to my heart, no matter how painful it may feel, so I can use the power of my voice to set others free.

*The strength to surrender brings you closer
to the freedom you seek.*

Life is about choosing to accept all of who

you are to unlock your inner mystery.

Masks

When I was twenty-three years old, I found myself in a psychologist's office, staring at the woman across from me. In what I can now say was not one of my finer moments, I yelled, "Fuck you, that is not possible! Who are you to tell me what I am? You are just a fucking wizard trying to ruin my life."

I'd just been diagnosed with major depressive disorder after being sent home from Brazil because of my relationship with alcohol and my manic episodes.

While temporary, my depressive periods were terrifying because I never knew when they would hit me. As a result, this created hardships in every area of my life.

After my best friend was killed in the Iraq War, I had unusual amounts of energy for months and functioned on only a few hours of sleep. It wasn't uncommon as a Marine to face bouts of depression after a traumatic event, but I started to engage in unusual behaviors (binge drinking coupled with lots of sex) and developed a dark sense of self.

There were days when I'd stare at the ceiling, contemplating life. I felt like I was in an alternate world, alone and stranded. Some days, I'd break down and flip out for no apparent reason. Other days I'd run for miles, crying.

I didn't know how to talk about it, so I got lost in this alternate world and began the battle of finding ways to end my life.

Depression makes you forget about everything else. Things that you would not usually do, you do. My dance with death began in this alternate world where I felt invincible.

In this world, I felt powerful. But I never had control. I started to dwell on my past. I felt guilty for many things, and I started talking about death. I knew something was off, but every day I kept dancing with death.

Sleep was nonexistent, but somehow I had energy. Training time turned to binge drinking, partying, and breaking curfew. Life was flashing before my eyes, and I had no clue what to do.

If you've ever served with me, you most likely saw me in this state of manic depression. All my impulsive and careless behaviors resulted from something I was fighting inside. When I was manic, I craved attention and felt indestructible. But I also had days where everything felt heavy and dark. It looked and felt like a hangover from repressed emotions that only seemed to lift when I was in this alternate world.

I fought this depression for more than a decade. I trained hard for a few hours a day. I ate whatever I wanted, drank a lot, functioned on a few hours of sleep, and didn't worry about my body. I became a workaholic while depression dominated every moment of my existence. The pain I felt inside surpassed any physical pain I endured. Yet, I never admitted this to anyone before writing this book.

Writing this still doesn't make sense to me. It sounds made up and like something that could've never happened to me. Maybe it's just another story inside my head, but all I know is that most days, I felt a vice squeezing every bit of energy out of me that made me want to end my life.

In Robert Masters' book, *To Be a Man,* he mentions how men, in general, are hurting far more than they show. Everyone pays the price for this as we numb our vulnerable emotions, resort to aggressive behavior and addiction, and take on multiple identities.

As I type these words, I wonder how many times and ways people felt unsafe with me around. My silent aggression created superficial guards for unresolved wounds, and the masks I wore protected all things vulnerable. They had me dancing around life like a puppet on strings being pulled and pushed in every direction.

These masks exist within each of us, feeding off our insecurities by tricking us into playing different acts in life. They create identities from our deepest wounds and take great pride in putting on a show. The more attached we are to the identities we hide behind, the more difficult and painful it becomes to reveal who we are underneath.

When I left the Marines, I spent no time considering the conflict of a lifelong struggle with an identity I had never fully resolved. I convinced myself that I was doing *fine* and started a family. I imagined it looked picturesque. But it felt dull and lackluster.

To me, life felt like a checklist. Marriage, fatherhood, and pursuing a big dream felt like tasks I needed to do. I had every reason to be grateful for life, but each day I sank deeper into a dark vault of depression. The worst part of it all, I had an amazing wife who believed in me, and I pushed her away as I drowned in a sea of unhealthy addictions, anger, and other distractions.

The isolation I felt—the financial pressure and the fatigue of holding it all together—reminded me of my childhood growing up. I felt trapped by the outside world as I watched familiar patterns of my past repeat in my life, and suicidal thoughts became a regular occurrence.

It's not that I wanted to die, but suicide seemed like a more honorable option than admitting I was the man who had created a massive chasm between my marriage. I was afraid of the man I was becoming, and the mask I wore convinced everyone I had it all together. Except I didn't; I never did.

I knew my marriage was falling apart, but I continued to live as if nothing mattered to me. Shame and guilt reinforced the distance from my wife, making me feel like a failed husband. As melodramatic as it seems, I was a warrior, and shame was an enemy I wasn't willing to face. I created masks to hide behind while I secretly began to plot the last act of my life without anyone ever knowing.

Planning your death is not an easy mask to hide behind, especially when you have a two-year-old daughter and a coaching career. But the Marines trained me well, and I put on an impressive act.

For almost a year, I fueled my life with adrenaline and focused on crafting an impressive physique that gained me more clients while beating myself up inside. I trained eight to ten clients a day and took on bodybuilding. At home, I thought about the ways I'd take my last breath.

I woke up at 3:30 a.m. every day and created a story in my head that went like this: *Our marriage is fine. I'll just tell everyone the long workdays and parenthood are a lot, so we agreed to take space. I'll keep telling people I'm seeing a therapist, and I'm doing great.*

Meanwhile, I felt the rage of a man with a broken heart. I felt guilty for everything that had happened, and the excruciating shame forced me to a place where I was ready to disappear. Taking my life was the only honorable way to end the pain and the easiest way to lift the burden I caused to others. One morning, after waking up late for work, I found myself in an empty parking lot with a photo of my daughter and a handgun. Suddenly, I had the gun inside my mouth, ready to leave this world.

That day is a blur, but the memories of everything I felt are not.

With my eyes closed, I tried to pull the trigger, but my fingers would not bend. It was as if I'd exposed a level of tenderness that numbed my entire body, and the gun fell to the floor beneath me.

I sat there in silence with my eyes closed, wondering if I was alive or not. At first, I thought I was dead. But the burning sensations running through my body and the tears falling down my cheeks signified I was very much alive. I opened my eyes, and the first thing I saw was the photo of my daughter staring back at me. The unconditional love from a three-year-old girl saved my life.

As I look back at my life over the last two decades, I can see a common theme among the many masks I wore. Camouflaged by stoicism, pride, and addictive behaviors, shame drove me deeper into depression as I separated myself from my heart and soul, and the man I desperately wanted to be.

I recognize that the most challenging thing I've ever done and will continue to do is live with an open heart. Chaos was all I knew, but the vulnerability I feel from taking off the masks is far less intense than the rules of masculinity that destroyed my life.

Today, I catch myself slipping into the man who wants to hold it all in. When I do, I remind myself of that day in my car. I know that nothing of value comes from closing off my heart to the world. The worst outcomes in my life all started with concealing who I really was and what I really thought. Without my vulnerability, I'm useless as a man, father, coach, and writer. My competitive nature and desire for physical strength are still a big part of my life, but I seek a different kind of power now. The real progress is harnessing the power to connect with parts of me once lost, and in these spaces, I am a dad, and nothing else matters.

I've fought long and hard against myself and others and now understand that the masks we wear drown out any chance for a connection to our hearts. This day will forever be my reminder that our hearts will always lead us to our truths every moment we are alive. All we have to do is find the courage to remove our masks and trust ourselves, no matter how vulnerable we may seem. When we do, the world will transform in front of us as our heart creates magnificent stories that light up any darkness in our way.

Now I write to release

the past. For I'm not

sure how long my

life will last.

One life, the same result

in the end. I welcome

death, he is my friend.

Wounds

It was as if my entire life stopped. Just like that, I was forced into the underworld and became a dark soul lost in a sea of heartbreak. No amount of military training could have prepared me for what the Greeks called the Katabasis: a point in a man's life where he must go through layers of repressed emotions and desires, and face the uncomfortable truths he's ignored while he descends into the dark shadows waiting for him.

Shortly after my separation, I found myself drawn to the shadows that lurked below. Darkness has been my companion for much of my life, but I faced something unfamiliar in the bottomless abyss. I grappled with sex, alcohol, and drugs to fuel my pain in the grueling underworld as my growing fascination with controlling my pain through intense sexual desires began.

I had a sense that my days would soon come to an end. The darkness that walked beside me now was beyond my control. He was no longer a companion, but an accomplice to my demise. A lifetime struggle with an identity crisis and depression created an intimate relationship with darkness himself. But I wasn't in this underworld to die (although, in a sense, part of me did). Instead, I lived out the desires of my pain. Instead of healing it, I gave into it. I played with the limits and boundaries of others' minds, bodies, and hearts.

At first, I felt ashamed of my desires. After feeling unworthy and rejected from my divorce, the first woman I met felt like an emotional storm for everything that needed to surface. I hadn't been with another woman in years, and I missed the sensation of another body against mine, but I didn't know who I was or trust myself, for the matter. I didn't know how to respond to the electric pulses deep within two lovers, and to my surprise, my cock was unresponsive to touch. My heart screamed at me, and my body desired to let go, but all I could do was sit there, lifeless, while darkness played a game with my mind and pulled at my heartstrings, leading me to an unfamiliar place.

I felt incredulous about what I saw in front of me: a clear door with no hinges, knob, or frame. On the other side, waiting for me, were endless lessons from wounds I needed to face. As I stepped between the spaces of both worlds, all those things I never thought I'd do in life, I did. I saw that my passage through the other side was contingent on my relationship to what was behind me, not in front of me.

I felt ashamed and rejected, and sex became a bandage for my wounds. I created a world where I felt in control. For three months, pain and pleasure fueled my passage to the other side. I dated women who enjoyed submitting. No feelings of unworthiness could touch me there. The sense of control gave me an altered state of consciousness that created a tremendous amount of trust with the women I met. Most of them had the exceptional qualities of a future partner, but I wasn't ready to let go.

At the same time, I created a magnificent art display inspired by the ties of heartbreak, submission, love, passion, lust, and intensity. I wanted to create a world for women to feel safe, and for me, it wasn't about rules and punishment; it was about empowerment—both for myself and the women who trusted me enough to submit. And what a powerful journey it was.

To see a woman silence her mind and body while I treated her like she was unbreakable was the only way I could understand the pain caused by my wounds. I needed these women in my life as much as they needed me. There was a great deal of intimacy, empathy, and intuition required during these relationships. The catharsis of control gave me the courage to turn inward, and what was waiting for me was a soul-affirming journey of celibacy.

Men's activist Robert Bly said, "Where a man's wound is, that is where his genius will be."

As I stepped through to the other side, I could look back and understand that my intense sexual desires and other addictions camouflaged my ability to let go. While this may have worked for a while, if I wanted complete freedom and control of my life, I had to go deeper. It was clear on this side that I existed in the underworld because I had no idea how to take responsibility for what I was feeling. The choice to go celibate was an opportunity to move closer to my heart and find my genius hidden in my desire to control others.

The only way to find my gift was to break free from these patterns. That meant no masturbation, sex, flirting, or dating. Celibacy revealed, for the first time in my life, the rawness of who I was as a man, stripped away from all distractions.

To my surprise, the nights of loneliness led to the creation of poems, articles, and this book. I started to appreciate and prefer my solitude. I didn't feel the need to escape. It wasn't enough to stop having sex; I am well disciplined by nature. I needed to break the connection between my sexuality and my feelings of manliness or masculinity. Sex needed to be about desire and connection, not my ego. I started by first learning how to develop an intimate connection to the wounds that led me to my destruction. And that meant letting it all go.

After the first month, I felt the power that came from being connected to my heart. I developed intimate friendships with women who came into my life during my celibacy journey who showed me that intimacy goes beyond sexual pleasure. They also showed me that I had so much love to give.

These days sex is not at the forefront of my mind, and I have enjoyed the privilege of getting to know women in the most profoundly intimate ways without ulterior motives. The entire experience of developing an intimate relationship with someone makes me feel vibrant and young again, which is empowering. Love is a fascinating subject to me because I don't believe I've even come close to fully feeling the depth of my heart and what I have to offer.

Walking through that door was one of the most powerful things I've ever done. It helped me remember the power of being fully connected to my heart and body. Most importantly, sex is a potent elixir for the soul's journey, and having control over my desires makes me a better man, lover, and creator.

Your skin against mine, I'm starving

with desire. Hypnotized by your love

my heart is on fire.

I look into your eyes and pull you close. I

create words of love and our bodies float.

Every curve and detail is not to be

overlooked. Here I will find what

boundaries to push.

In between the sheets is where

I learn to let go. Love has no limits

In this space I flow.

Shape-Shifters

When we watch the world change shape unexpectedly, we hold onto everything we can for any sense of control. For the majority of my life, holding on to the only story I knew created a sense of comfort. In a way, it helped me survive.

I thought this story was the only way to live, so I abandoned myself without even considering the possibility of change. When I finally stepped outside the box I lived in, I came face to face with the underlying beliefs that stood in my way. It hurt. But as my tears came, I was finally able to go deeper to change my life.

I spent so much time looking outside myself for something that didn't exist, that fear blinded me from seeing what I'd created. So I took a new shape. I let go of the identities that didn't serve me. I struggled at first as I fought the tears that needed to surface. But I gave myself permission to allow the pain to come through by trusting myself in the unknown. I learned to recognize where shame weighed me down, and worked with the years of numbing while I watched shame turn into a beautiful gift.

These words I've written are how I let go and took a new shape. They remind me I am human.

Shallow breaths turn to full exhales and time

slows down in the moments you write

frantically watching words bleed

from darkness within.

I chose to break the mold and show my daughter that there is no right or wrong way to live her life. That she can experience all kinds of shapes in life that the external world might deem dysfunctional or failures, but she can choose to see them differently.

Wayne Dyer said, "When you change the way you look at things, the things you look at change." He's telling us that **if we remove the masks, find genius from our wounds, and shift our perspective, we can set ourselves free and watch the world morph into something greater than we could have ever imagined.**

Uncertainty is everywhere, and the longer we fight the unknown, the longer we remain trapped between the past and the future. Once grounded, our lives will morph into something that flies. If we don't look at the tensions we've created and the things flying away, we'll find ourselves in limbo, further from ourselves and constantly worrying about something we can't control.

I've worn masks and shields, bluffed, and resisted the changes taking shape, and it cost me everything. I've learned that our stories are ever-changing, and we can't find our gift in life if we resist what is trying to unfold. We can choose to see the changes as something we fear or as a calling from deep within our hearts and souls.

I have fought a long, ancient battle. I was a warrior with heavy armor that guarded my authentic self, and I never saw the shapes for what they were—life lessons. When I finally allowed my heart to open up to everything I feared, my body felt lighter, and I became the creator of the life I wanted. I learned to trust that if I am the one who gives meaning to everything, then I am also the one who can change the meaning at any time.

Today, I change shapes eagerly. I flow between worlds of creativity, darkness, and love with no preconceived ideas of what I am in these moments or what I need. I've seen what happens to others when life takes another form unexpectedly in front of their eyes. I know what it feels like to pretend to be someone you're not. These spaces prevent us from adapting. We only recycle what we know rather than listen to the shapes our hearts want to create. We do not need more humans to be afraid of change. We need more humans who are willing to let their walls down and shift into whatever makes them feel aligned with the life they are worthy of creating.

I will continue to change shape for the rest of my life. To embrace these shifts is one of the hardest things I've ever had to do. But I'd rather listen to my heart than get weighed down by beliefs that don't give me the freedom to flow freely.

This book is a powerful reminder of how much we can change in the face of uncertainty. In the middle of a worldwide pandemic, my words shapeshifted into the form of a mentor. Every day I wrote about my life, others reached out to me about how aligned they felt with their hearts. It was powerful to witness what I helped create. To see how every breath, word, and interaction form something new and allow us to walk into the places we feared together. If I had never taken off my masks or found writing to take me to the edge, who knows if I'd be here today.

Shapeshifting allows me to see how supported I am in the unknown. When something falls away, I must not forget that I am human and to look inward for the courage to let go of what I've lost and find another shape taking place. My goal is to surrender to change because change is constant, no matter where we are in life. I'm finally learning to stop running after something that is already gone. I will continue to shapeshift and take risks beyond anything I've ever experienced till my last breath. I will meet you here; we all will.

⌒⌒

Now is the time to explore what you had a part in creating

These words morph into something greater that is waiting

With your breath as your companion to provide you with space

Let your walls come down and

See the changes taking place

MENTORS

Love is a gatekeeper
    to freedoms we seek. We will
        need courage and strength
            to listen to our heart whenever it speaks.

We must never stop dancing, for
    the key to our freedoms lies within
        our heart's center. Love is not blind.
           It's life's most precious mentor.

Mountains

It's forty-one degrees, and I'm 5,300 feet up in the Appalachian Mountains with no one around but the north, south, west, and east winds calling me to connect deeper to my heart. The leaves are changing, and the silence is a gentle reminder of the power of nature. The arduous trails ahead remind me of what it means to breathe, live, and feel connected to parts of me I lost long ago.

At the top of the mountain, I let out a primal scream and feel the release of the identities and roles I've been carrying. I've been sober for eighteen months, and I've had some fascinating revelations after challenging myself to be uncomfortable. Spending time in nature inspires significant changes in my psyche. Nature is the source of our well-being, and traveling to her can give us the strength to reach beyond things more powerful than ourselves.

I've trained myself to connect deeper by challenging myself in the unknown. Up here, I can't pretend to be someone I'm not. The fifty miles per hour winds remind me to move with intent and connect with my warrior spirit deep within. My deep breaths and the sharpness in my movements signify that I am changing with the seasons too. My heart is my greatest ally, and every conscious step and breath restore what was once lost and broken.

Everything that appears to be cracked and broken

beneath your feet is a puzzle and a process

of life that you will continually meet.

With your courageous will and strong heart

take a deep breath because without any

effort you will see all that has fallen begins to stand.

When I think about feeling lost, broken, or unseen and what others have shared with me, I see that we all create an impressive work of art. Each of us has a unique set of eyes that can create stories with a face others adore. A voice that inspires others to transform. Lips that can kiss, and a tongue that can taste. It's a beautiful experience that tends to go to waste.

Along the way, someone told us we had to be more than what we needed. So, we forgot to love, laugh, breathe, dance, cry, and experience life for what it is. But at any given moment, the storms of life can come. They remind us that nothing in life is ever certain. And that it takes great determination and strength to connect with your heart and feel the height of the human experience.

I come to the mountains to find myself again. The path I honor comes in many forms and is one of the most remarkable experiences I grant myself as a human. No more. No less.

If you're experiencing discomfort, pain, or suffering, or are uncertain about who you are, it's a sign that you are very much alive. It's all here to help you embrace uncertainty, and change with gentle submission. There is no room in the world for pretending they do not exist. You are not broken. You are human.

Take a few deep breaths to see that your body holds the keys to all the freedoms you seek. No matter what war we may be facing, we can always return to our hearts; we can always connect with our breath.

I choose to feel. My words will forever be a reminder of my wounds and the invitation life has offered me.

Breathe, write, cry, and play.

This is my life.

I wouldn't have it any other way.

Love

Several months into my sobriety, one of my mentors asked me, "When was the last time you looked at yourself in the mirror and said, 'I love you'?" My stomach dropped. I felt my heart scream at me behind the walls of heartbreak and fought to hold back the tears running down my cheeks.

She went on to say, "You are looking for something that is not lacking. You give your love to others in hopes to heal what aches. While the pain you are experiencing is deep, have you ever considered that the sense of emptiness you feel is because you separated yourself from your heart a long time ago?"

Up until that point, I hadn't thought about love that way. It was as if I'd left the love I felt for myself behind to fill what felt hollow.

I went into the bathroom after our conversation and looked at myself in the mirror. This time, I didn't see a thousand-yard stare or a lost, lonely boy, but a glimpse into the soul of a grounded man with integrity and an open heart. As I held my gaze and continued to breathe deeply, I realized what I seek in others is fundamentally mine to own first. **I put a hand on my heart and realized that our suffering can never be defeated or washed away but only transformed when we explore the love we have for ourselves first.**

When I tended to the places I'd ignored for so long, darkness turned to light, and there was nothing more I needed to discover. I only needed to feel the abundance of love around me. At the center of my repressed emotions was the human experience.

Throughout the next year, I listened to the rhythm of my heart every morning I got up to write this book. Amid my writing malaise, darkness came, but each visit was shorter than the last. I was learning to love myself through the exploration of a being creator, father, and lover. Every conversation and story transformed the world in front of me. My doubts and fears dissipated, and my love expanded past limits I never knew existed.

I know what it feels like to walk down roads you're unsure of while your heart screams to you from a distance. How exhausting it feels to hold it all together as life seems to escape your tired eyes. I know the suffering that comes from witnessing the separation of the heart. For a long time, shadows walked alongside me while I frantically looked for the light to return, and lost myself in the process. Today, I finally see that maybe the point of life isn't what we thought it was.

Why do we give so much love to others instead of learning to love ourselves first? I look around the world and see so many people searching for something outside themselves, hiding behind the world's busyness, disconnected from their hearts. **But all this denying who we are eventually leads to the same result—death.**

I've learned to make space for what needs to come through. To do that, I have to let my heart speak without shame or judgment.

Usually, it's first thing in the morning after meditation, or when my daughter isn't staying with me. It's a time when I give myself a safe space to drop out of my head and into my body while journaling on the following prompts: **"What is the truth I'm avoiding in this struggle?" "What do I gain from holding on to this old story?" "What is possible for me if I let go?" "In what ways can I show myself compassion during this struggle?" "What do I need most right now?"**

This saves me from losing myself at the expense of something or someone. It also prevents me from recycling my hurt to my daughter or anyone else. In shifting my perspective, I strengthen my heart's muscles while love fills every part of my existence. When my inspiration feels dry, I take a deep breath and listen to my heart. One of the greatest gifts we can give ourselves is this listening, one beat at a time, as we allow our hearts to open up to all we fear as we connect with ourselves to find deeper meaning.

Today, I float between worlds of darkness and light because I know each serves its purpose. Between these worlds is my ever-evolving capacity to love freely with no limits. When conditions arise or change unexpectedly, I remind myself to take a deep breath, close my eyes, and sit in this space with no judgment and let the process of life unfold. If I sit here long enough, time slows down, and my words give me the courage to release identities that do not serve me. What transforms in front of me is ancient, and the vulnerability that lies here is more satisfying than anything external.

Follow the deep, unwavering wisdom of your heart.

It knows who you are inside in case you forgot.

The Body

I'm writing this chapter while I sip on a fancy cup of coffee after a ten-mile run in the rain during a global pandemic. I move every day. From morning rituals that include breathwork and light mobility exercises to yoga and strength training, movement is part of my life.

My willingness to try new things and get curious about how they make me perform has always fascinated me. From endurance races, powerlifting, bodybuilding, and everything in between, I trained hard for hours, ate, drank, and functioned on a few hours of sleep, and didn't worry about my body. But there was a double-edged sword to that life: I had self-confidence issues, I was in and out of the emergency room for years with a medical condition no one could figure out, and I was sick more times than I can remember.

Right after I realized I was getting divorced, I went into Marine mode. Flashbacks and nightmares became a regular occurrence, and sleep was nonexistent as thoughts of my wife with another man kept me on edge. I tried to control my life by fueling my early mornings with four a.m. workouts. But those weren't enough, and I pushed my body to new extremes with Brazilian Ji Jitsu and CrossFit.

Angry at my wife and disgusted with myself, I existed on pure adrenaline. I felt the constant need to prove to everyone that I was worthy of life itself. I spent hours staying active as I bounced between clients and pushed my body to new limits. Exhaustion emptied me, and sometimes I'd fall asleep in my car and wake up late for clients.

One morning, after a heavy training session, my body shut down. I went to grab a quick snack before my next client, and I couldn't swallow or breathe. The excruciating pain in my chest was so bad that I vomited for an entire hour. As you might have guessed, I was immediately rushed to the hospital. As I sat there in the hospital bed alone, a team of doctors walked in and explained how stress was eating away my insides. That day, one of my most profound revelations was also one of the most difficult to wrap my mind around. As counterintuitive as it seems, I wasn't as healthy as I thought.

I existed on the surface. I stayed in a constant state of tension thanks to the incredible distrust I had for everyone. The years of extremes I'd put my body through caused an imbalance to my nervous system and my digestive tract, resulting in large amounts of inflammation in my esophagus. My constant trips to the hospital showed how an extreme athlete like myself was no match for what my body was telling me to do—slow down.

I look back at all my hospital visits and think about how stress was synonymous with who I was. Most of the time, I never thought twice about the chaos surrounding me because I was a Marine. It strikes me that the same protective mechanisms I built also kept me in a perpetual state of anxiety that caused havoc on my body. I never knew where the off switch was. Even if I had, I wouldn't have been able to use it. My pain and the trauma of my past didn't have an off switch, so neither did I.

Since then, I've met a variety of people who know how to find a balance between it all. From strongmen and Cross-fitters to martial artists, endurance athletes, and yogis, they all showed me how to observe my body on a deeper level. As a result, I altered my sleep patterns and nutritional habits, connected to my breath, pushed my body to extremes, and the medical problems I had for over a decade haven't come back. None of it was easy.

As I went through my journey, many people asked me how I did it. I think about all the questions I received during some of my darkest days while I appeared to have it all together. And that excites me because humans out there want to observe their bodies on a deeper level.

But those questions about diets and training are just the tip of the iceberg when it comes to mastering our bodies.

From the outside, it may look like we've made massive leaps forward in the realm of human performance, but little of this is useful if we don't take the step of slowing down. If anything, the lifestyle we find ourselves in today forces us to live on the notion of diets, exercise, and quick fixes to make the health and fitness industry billions of dollars without yielding results.

The challenge with letting our health depend on the two pillars of diet and exercise without considering the external factors responsible for how we show up to the world is that it makes it easier for us to blame others instead of going deeper. In the grand scheme of things, we're hardly scratching the surface of going deeper with our bodies.

So how can we master our bodies? How can we take a step back and accept these inconvenient truths? How can we slow down to see there is so much more to mastering our bodies than surface-level looks?

Slowing down is a strange claim for a Marine who spent much of his life pushing his body to extremes, but here's how I see it:

If we want to master our bodies, we must learn how to shift from the abstract to more focus. If we want to feel more congruent with our personalities and more grounded in our stress, we must see our body as a protector, not something superficial.

Before we can do all this, we must learn how to travel through the chaos that disconnected us from ourselves in the first place.

Luxurious lifestyles, stable food supplies, and social media feeds with information at our fingertips make it easy to avoid slowing down. Building an identity around the stress in your life leads you to become one with the frenzy, and disconnected from your body. Everyday life is a grind, performance flatlines, relationships end, health declines, and we become a hamster on the wheel of life. This repetitive cycle robs us of our ability to explore our bodies on a deeper level because it feels impossible to slow down. But I can assure you that beyond this superficial layer is another version of yourself, a self that is more confident, surefooted, and healthier than anything you could have imagined.

If you want to connect deeper with your body, and aren't sure where to start, do not be afraid of the challenges you face. Stand directly in front of them and begin the task of figuring it out for yourself. Connecting deeper with your body doesn't occur only through exercise and nutrition. It's your consistent effort to keep going. It's an accumulation of your efforts and how you show up to the world every day, even when life pushes you back. It's a skill that requires a lot of patience because you have to learn to accept yourself. If you never accept all of who you are, you'll never be able to appreciate your body. You'll use your body to fuel your suffering like I did. But you don't have to. Liberation from your suffering comes from acceptance.

The fear and avoidance of the unknown will keep you stranded from your most authentic self. Each time you observe your body on a deeper level, you'll learn more about trusting yourself to be steady during the chaos of life. Your willingness to keep showing up every day on a deeper level will give you unique superpowers to take on some of life's most difficult transitions. And when you get past the noise in life, you will see something greater than you ever could have imagined.

I still train hard these days, but you'll also find me doing yoga, meditating, and taking more rest days than I ever have in my entire life. I have to because I never want to go back, and I believe I am just getting started mastering my body. It's not about superficial looks anymore, nor is my body a place to store years of repressed emotions and prove others wrong. To me, my body is an extension of my soul, and guides me along my journey. I know that my body is only mine for a short time on Earth, and it is completely separate from who I am. I focus on listening to my body when it speaks and learning to trust myself in the unknown because only I can take myself where I want to go.

Remember now, this wisdom deep within your soul

*Listen to your body when it speaks, it will
show you what you need to grow*

Gravity

One morning, after drowning myself in a sea of alcohol
and waking up to a woman I cared nothing about,
I thought about my daughter going on without me in
life and wondered, *What the fuck just happened? How did
I become the man I said I'd never become?*

I knew I needed to figure things out for my daughter's sake, so I
headed to the gym to clear my head. As I searched for music, on
my feed appeared a TED Talk by a middle-aged bald man who'd
made pain his guru. Intrigued by what he had to say, I left the gym
and turned up the volume. I sat in the grass outside, listening
to his story of twenty-eight days in darkness after a divorce that
challenged him to slow down in life.

His name was Traver Boehm, and I was on the phone with him
the next week. It all seemed a bit crazy to me. He wasn't the first
man to talk about life after divorce, but the way he spoke of the

Divine and Primal integration and the path of an Uncivilized Man left me grounded and calm after our conversation.

A month after hiring Traver to coach me through my divorce, I was sober, celibate, and meditating daily. He showed me superpowers I never knew existed. One of those superpowers was breathing. Traver recommended a retreat based on intentional breathwork. I'd messed around with some postural breathing courses as a performance coach to reduce sympathetic tone in the body and taken some yoga classes, but this breathing was a hack into my nervous system and something I'd never experienced before. Before I knew it, I was on a plane to Colorado about to "defy gravity" and find out how the breath would become an influential mentor in my life.

When I landed at the Denver airport, I met three strangers from completely different walks of life. Skeptical of what was to come, at best, I thought everyone was a hippie. I rented a car, and we drove three hours through the Colorado mountains to a mansion in Steamboat. The drive was incredible, and my skepticism slowly lifted as our conversations sparked new hope inside me.

When we arrived at the mansion, we were greeted with warm hugs from Traver and Leila, a spiritual coach. To my surprise, a few people already knew each other, which confirmed my original thoughts on the days ahead. *"Defy Gravity?" Who do these people think they are? They don't know who I am or what I've been through.*

How can these humans promise me a breakthrough with something as simple as breathing?

The place was massive and offered a variety of options to keep us occupied. From an indoor pool with three floors and plenty of rooms to give us private space when needed, I felt like I was on MTV Cribs. But we weren't there for a vacation. One of the women I drove there with knew Leila, and she became my best friend over the next few days. "Come with an open heart and mind, and the next few days will be incredible," she told me while sharing how transformational Leila's courses were.

I unpacked and grabbed a journal to collect my thoughts before we started for the evening. I didn't know why, but I wrote the words *just breathe* and drew a heart around them, which sent a burst of emotions through my body. I even let out a few tears. What I saw after that was like nothing I'd ever experienced before.

After a long day, we all came together and sat down for an opening circle. Here, Leila and Traver told us to set intentions for the next few days as they explained the retreat theme, "Defy Gravity." In a world filled with heartbreak and disappointment, we would soon learn to silence our inner critics and shed layers of emotional armor. To do that, I would have to face many demons and open my heart to the world.

We exited the circle and sat down for dinner together. I noticed everyone seemed to open up quickly, but I sat silently for most of the night. This was the first time I'd been around others who were so open to life. My heart was still closed. Although the first evening was awkward for me, the next few days became a safe space for me to take off my armor and show my wounds.

During that restless first night, I went to the gym at 3:30 a.m. I threw in my headphones and started to deadlift. It was a hard training session, and I could feel the weights clinking as I pushed my body to its limit. Oblivious to the house's set-up, I noticed a figure in the corner of the window; it was Leila. Apparently, I had woken up the entire house with the banging of the weights. I apologized for being loud, put away the weights, and plunged myself into the pool. Later that morning, in front of the group, I was told I could not lift, run, or perform any strenuous activities while I was on the retreat. It was time to take off my armor by sitting with everything I did not want to feel.

The mornings consisted of meditation, journaling, and yoga. The afternoons and evenings were filled with deep, soul-cleansing work that prepared us for intense breathwork sessions in the coming days. I thought I went to the retreat to move through my divorce. Little did I know I would confront the repressed emotions that had led to me wearing heavy armor for over a decade. Leila and Traver walked us through shadow work, a concept I was unfamiliar with, and how it manifests in our lives without us realizing it; that is, we create an alternate identity from past trauma in our lives. As a result, we hide behind our shadows while turning away from the issues we need to face, which prevents us from showing up to the world with an open heart.

Although the first few days were awkward and painful for me, true to what Traver mentioned before coming to the retreat, I felt lighter. With every conversation and moment of silent reflection, my emotional armor slowly came off. On the third day, we were no longer strangers, and it was time to defy gravity.

Twenty of us laid face-up, soon to let go of the weight sitting heavily on our shoulders. Leila and Traver told us to close our eyes and start with a few simple breaths to calm our nervous systems and prepare our bodies. Most of us had no clue what to expect, and I was skeptical about this entire experience.

I heard the others exhale and release, but my mind raced a million miles a minute, and I couldn't let go. I heard the sounds of our bodies move together rhythmically, as our breathing controlled the presence of the room. Off in the distance, I heard a voice say, "Take two quick inhales, then a quick exhale, and keep repeating until you feel warm. Whatever you do, trust the process and do not stop." I resisted the urge to stop, and the intensity of our breathing dissolved the room around me. I lost myself in the experience. I clenched my fists, and my entire body burned with aggression.

Leila came over to me and put her hands on my heart. Leila has made breathwork a central part of her life. While most of her work has focused on yoga and trauma coaching with women, she's no stranger to getting a man who's hidden behind years of pain to surrender to the breath and let go. She's good at it.

Within a few minutes of her calming presence, something happened inside my body, and I let go. The room turned black, splashes of vibrant colors come across my eyelids, and tears rushed down my face. I took a few more powerful breaths, and I saw vivid images of my best friend getting killed by a roadside bomb in Iraq. I clenched my entire body and began to scream in pain. The deep breathing had triggered a response that resembled the experience people report when engaged in hallucinations; I felt like I was in Iraq, watching him die.

Of course, I was right there on my mat. I felt the falsity of my identities working desperately to hold on and let go with every exhale, and I had a raging fit. I don't recall exactly what happened in the moment, but I do remember Traver removing me to the other side of the room in concern for myself and others' safety.

After our session, I felt high from the breathwork. Without realizing it, I left the mansion and walked around like a mindless zombie in the middle of nowhere without anyone knowing. The breathing induced an expanded consciousness and spiritual insight that made me feel like I was floating in another world.

I'm not sure how long I was gone, and I know that walk was irresponsible of me, but I never felt more loved and accepted by the world at that moment. After the group found me, I returned to the mansion to share my experience with the others, and all I could do was stand there and cry.

Looking back, my experience with breathwork makes sense. When I could finally breathe deeply, I hacked into my nervous system and accessed the parts of my life that had been restricted by years of repressed emotions. With my breath as my guide, I could see all the ways I had distanced myself from my heart.

Breathe in, zoom out.
Breathe out, zoom in—no different you
and I, in retrospect, the same.

Fighting through the darkness, we are all
connected through the pain.

Take a deep breath to find your way back to the center.

Here you will see your breath is a faithful
companion in your adventure.

The Edge

Writing takes me to the edge in life. The separation and alienation I feel from myself merge with my deepest desires to feel seen and heard. Words form in the shape of a mentor, teaching me that we are very much the same even though we're all different on the outside. In my most vulnerable moments, I reach a threshold where I can listen closely to the moments in which I seek to escape. Every word allows me to sink deeper and feel the present moment take shape as I fight to connect to my heart and heal what was accidentally scarred and broken.

Your edge in life doesn't need to include writing, training hard, or some insane adventure. It waits for you wherever fear, pain, grief, and shame keep you hidden behind masks and shadows. Those places can find you in everyday life, even in the most mundane places.

I've never told anyone this before, but most days, I wake up early because I have weird dreams. I suspect my ex-wife knew about these dreams because I'd wake up with night terrors, but she never knew what they were about.

Most of the dreams are a blur of me caught between the past, present, and future.

The more I tried to hide my dreams, the more vivid my dance with darkness became. Shame, guilt, and remorse created an image of the Grim Reaper himself.

His hood covers his eyes

In the distance, an axe ready to hack

Running on an endless track

Nowhere to go

The price of running is my soul

I once did everything I could to run from this, but today I write. I feel the two sides of me fighting to reach the edge. My body urges my hand to move my pen in honesty and truth. That connection signifies that something is stirring deep within my heart and soul.

Out on the edge, waiting for me with an outstretched hand is the wild man who longs for adventures. His desires are fueled by masculine power and driven by shame. He's a warrior and fights the world with fear over love because it's all he knows. Stoic and charismatic, he is cold, frozen in time, and distances himself from anyone who tries to get close.

Then there is the creator. He finds the courage to connect the primal and the divine. He craves the gentle touch of her lips against his because he knows how important it is to have a strong woman by his side. For him, inspiration is more potent than a closed-off heart.

A richness exists when the two selves collide. And since I am the writer of my own story, I can embrace the emerging landscape that gives me the space I need to create a life worth living. Hope and possibility open my core wounds as the edge brings light to my life where darkness once grew.

Some people look at me and think I'm crazy. Others look at me with disdain. And some look at me in complete admiration. To that, I say, *Choose to go deeper than a life lived with suffering and sorrow. Do not fear your edge because you may not live tomorrow.*

In my short life, I've learned that the edge is where I want to be. It's often uncomfortable, scary, painful, and lonely. I find hidden versions of myself there, stronger than before I trusted myself to write. My writing calls me to leave my comfort zone and surrender to the unknown with an open heart.

I've lived a life afraid of the edge. I recognize when others walk down roads of emptiness, fearful of what they might meet out there in the unknown. I see the faces of others trapped behind the past and future, far from the present. I know the anger and aggression in a man who is desperately trying to hold on while his heart screams at him every night, telling him to let go. I feel the pain of a woman who makes love to a man with an empty heart.

I understand your pain because when the world is fast asleep, I relive it all. I feel my heart beating as the shadows try to pull me deep, but words lift the heaviness. They allow me to let go. The not-so-gentle reminder of my past always calls me. But the pain fades when I move closer to the edge. I guess that's why they say crying is both painful and beautiful at the same time.

When I feel the urge to run from everything, writing reminds me that the truths to the freedoms I seek are out there on the edge. With no judgment, the edge brings me home. As my words heal my wounds, they also heal the hearts of others. That's scary to think, write, and see. But it's also freeing, and I wouldn't have it any other way.

*As life ceases to comfort you, see that
within every struggle is a choice.*

Out there on the edge, you will find courage in your voice.

All the places you run from are home to the freedoms you seek.

*Run no longer my friend, the edge is where
you find something unique.*

THE LAST BREATH

Perched above my experiences in life, I held my heart ever so gently

It was all so simple I whispered to my lover, here is my last entry

We came to this earth to feel, love, and be more than we
can imagine

Yet, so many of us neglect to listen to our hearts and show
ourselves compassion

Eyes that can see into a world filled with inspiration and love

Arms created to hold a gentle embrace like the presence of a dove

A heart that follows a rhythm to remind us we are very much alive

A voice so powerful it transforms and empowers others to survive

We forget about the simplicity in life as we use our own minds
to experience a war

Our breath is the key to life, don't forget to return to it when
you need to explore

When life seems torn apart to pieces and all feels lost

Every choice we make comes with a consequence, a price for
a thought

When darkness comes, and it will find us on the days we least expect

We must not resist, but find our hearts and discover how to connect

When in this dark space, do not focus on the challenge, but
look for good

Explore the possibilities in front of us, all that hurts is often
misunderstood

Pain is a process of life in which we must dig deeper to see

The gift of light will always come back if we turn inward and
wait patiently

The present moment we are living is the point of life in which
we all seek

*We are always being heard, the Universe listens to the words
   we speak*

*Endless opportunities are right in front of us if we open up our
   eyes and ears*

*The path we all need to walk down is hidden behind a deep
   forest of fears*

We must not forget to close our eyes and sit with this moment

*Nothing is more valuable than realizing we are our greatest
   opponent*

*You came into this world to live and be more than you
   can imagine*

*If given the chance, listen to your heart more because that is
   where magic will happen*

I lay here today and feel the power of my last breath

*I am not afraid of the end, I accept and surrender to my new
   friend, his name is death*

The Last Entry

When I began writing this book, my dad let my family know he was slowly dying of cancer. The disease spread into his bones and is eating away at his insides. Seeing him live through the process has been one of the most painful experiences to watch from afar. I have seen a lot of death in life, but watching him surrender to something he cannot control is a powerful reminder that our last breath can come at any time.

If we look at our experiences from this viewpoint, our last breath becomes a potent elixir to fuel our darkest and brightest days.

Except sometimes, it's hard to think about our experiences that way. Some days I write and watch my heart and soul bleed out on the pages of my life. Pain, death, depression, and betrayal are the antagonists of my story. But they are also the fire that fuels my creativity. This led me to the question I've addressed several times in this book: **If the end is death, and this is life, what am I searching for?**

Alan Watts said that most of us talk to ourselves all day long to never face reality.

That is to say, we hold our stagnant memories of the past and worries about the future in our short, shallow breaths. As such, we're unable to welcome new opportunities. But what if we searched a bit deeper and filled our lungs with air as if it was our last breath? We might find a completely new life emerging. This is how we shed layers of ourselves. This is the gift of life, how we see what we need, and why the breath is so powerful.

We always have the power to breathe until we don't. We can choose to see that everything we endure serves as a vehicle to an expanded version of ourselves, or we can decide to suffocate the spaces in our bodies that need to breathe with anxiety and stress. Either way, we are all part of a brilliant transformation occurring at this moment as we collectively search to find truth and liberation from our suffering.

From this place of awareness, no matter the pain we feel, we can return to our breath and see it as a framework for what is possible. All the experiences I've written about are somehow my last breaths. Depression, divorce, and identity struggles are the fears that held my ribs down with cold, rigid fingers, and I lost myself in the stagnant breaths of yesterday. This tension made me feel lost, unloved, and like a failure even while writing.

Until my dad hit our family with the news of his sickness. His time left here on earth inspired me to reevaluate my relationship with the world. And while my experiences may be a bit extreme, I can say that each step I take forward today, no matter what landscape emerges, is a chance to create a new story. It all starts with taking another breath. I've cut the ties with the fears that once suffocated my body. I'm happy and healthy because I surrendered to the fact that we will take our last breaths.

People like my dad understand the power of the last breath. They do not fear death but instead live as if something new is being born. This dance with death gives them the courage to continue living with an open heart and surrender to whatever is unfolding. Fear is useless in this dance; trusting yourself is paramount.

Our last breath doesn't mean we stop trying to live, or give up in the face of adversity; it means we surrender to the ideas or beliefs that prevent us from being able to breathe fully. When we accept the idea of our last breath, we can rest easy knowing we're on our way to transcending into something greater than ourselves.

Sometimes it takes deep suffering to see there is a great life force supporting us. Our pain is often needed for our soul's expansion. I witnessed this when I saw my dad cry for the first time. It took thirty-five years for me to see him cry. But I believe the tears he sheds today are his way of clearing a path for his soul's calling. Every tear stitches together the divide we created between ourselves a long time ago.

To see him endure chemotherapy and take daily medications is a not-so-subtle reminder that my last breath will eventually come no matter what journey I'm on.

One of my mentors once told me, "Though we are all different on the outside, we are all together in spirit. Underneath our scars lies a universal truth." I didn't know what she meant at the time, but I can rest easy today seeing the truth she was talking about. We must learn to live with the fact that our last breaths will always come.

We might not need to stare darkness in the face or think about death as if this could be our final moments. Rather, we need to resist the temptation to resent, hate, fear, or control when we are in deep suffering because that will only suffocate our chances to breathe. If we can find the courage to sit with the discomfort, even if only for a moment, then we can find liberation in taking our last breath to expand into something waiting for us on the exhale.

I'm not going to say that I'm always grounded because I know facing stress can't be avoided. But these days, I choose to remember the power of my last breath and how it can clear the path for my soul's calling.

Wake up, feet on the ground.

The floor is a reminder you have been granted another day.

Breathe to connect with your heart.

Notice the stillness in your breath.

You are here.

Not there.

You are very much alive.

The Last Hand

I guess this is the part of the book where I tie everything together. I'm supposed to bring everything I've learned into a pithy statement you can use to improve your life. Well, since words are what healed my heart and soul, I'm going to leave you with something I wrote about shuffling the cards of life.

Exhausted from trying to outrun my past

I want to be free, it's time to act fast.

I got lost in the bottle that forced me to hide behind masks—
numbed by addictions that never gave me the
courage to tell anyone how I felt.

Five hundred and forty days later, sober words give me the
strength to shuffle the cards of life I've been dealt.

Straight flush, five cards, all in a sequence.

The power of love exposed my weakness.

A memorable hand caused my identity to intertwine.

I could never see it because the cards of life played with my mind.

A broken heart offers a superpower beyond something greater than I can see. Freedom is here, in these words I speak.

Despite everything I've endured, I still find myself standing in front of the mirror, shedding the layers of myself hidden behind limiting beliefs and old stories. My heart fights to stay open, and when depression pulls me deep on those days, I give life everything I have to take another step forward. Like you, my thoughts wander when I find myself trapped between the past and the future, far from the present. These days, I don't run from those feelings but instead use them as a reminder that I am alive and experiencing more than ever what it's like to be a human being rather than a human doing.

Thich Nhat Hanh said, "Before we can make deep changes in our lives, we have to look into our diet, our way of consuming. We have to live in such a way that we stop consuming the things that poison us and intoxicate us. Then, we will have the strength to allow the best in us to arise, and we will no longer be victims of anger, of frustration."

In other words, we must first learn to uncover what we hide beneath that caused us to be disconnected from ourselves in the first place. By writing this book, I have set forth a powerful unfolding—a space for you to open your heart so truths can shine from places of darkness.

The shadows of my past sit with me, but the light of my presence shines through dark caverns previously untouched. I avoided this path for years, and these pages prove that no matter how painful things may seem, something better is waiting for you when you see that you have nowhere to go in life but to be here in this moment.

I'm not here because I think I'm better than you. Nor did I write this book to get lost on a shelf somewhere in the busyness of life. I wrote this book to prove to you (and myself) that we are never in control of our lives. But we can control our freedom. You and I are both free. We don't have to be victims of the unconscious battle between our inner and outer worlds. By doing the necessary work, I've found hidden gems in my deepest wounds and think of life differently now. Especially when the world is fast asleep, and I write frantically as my heart bleeds out what no one can take from me: the truth.

My heart is free today, knowing that you, too, are free. As you go through your life, remember to create space for yourself to breathe deeply, connect to your heart, and move with your body. These things will provide you with solace when life feels heavy.

On the days you feel heavy and lost, remember that no one is coming to save you. In moments of doubt, you need to find the strength to save yourself. When the world is fast asleep, there is courage deep within your soul. It is here that you will find something greater than yourself—an invitation to be and feel more than you could have ever imagined. Every tough transition ignites a flame of passion for finding your voice and emerging stronger than before. It's an amazing feeling when you finally realize your growth matters, and you don't need anyone to confirm who you are meant to be.

This is my last hand

My words create cards

that only new stories command.

Still fighting

Still writing

I let the tears fall.

Each verse reminds me tears

are the greatest gift of being alive through it all.